PHP
Pocket Reference

Rasmus Lerdorf

Beijing • Cambridge • Farnham • Köln • Paris • Sebastopol • Taipei • Tokyo

PHP Pocket Reference

by Rasmus Lerdorf

Published by O'Reilly & Associates, Inc., 101 Morris Street, Sebastopol, CA 95472.

Editor: Paula Ferguson

Production Editor: Colleen Gorman

Cover Design: Ellie Volckhausen

Printing History:

January 2000:   First Edition

1-56592-769-9
[C]

[3/00]

Table of Contents

PHP Pocket Reference

Introduction

PHP is a server-side, HTML-embedded, cross-platform scripting language—quite a mouthful. In simpler terms, PHP provides a way for you to put instructions in your HTML files to create dynamic content. These instructions are read and parsed by the web server; they never actually make it to the browser that is displaying the page. The web server replaces your PHP code with the content that the code was written to produce.

PHP can be configured to run either as a server module or as a standalone CGI script. At the time of this writing, the server-module version is only production-ready for the Apache web server on Unix systems. The CGI version runs with all web servers on both Unix and Windows 95/98/NT. On the Windows platform (as of PHP Version 4), the server module is being developed to work with ISAPI, NSAPI, and WSAPI, which means the server module will eventually work with Microsoft's IIS, Netscape's Enterprise Server, and O'Reilly's WebSite. See *http://www.php.net* for availability details.

The PHP language itself borrows concepts from other common languages, such as C and Perl. If you have some experience with one of these languages, you should feel right at home with PHP. In addition to the core language, PHP provides a wide variety of functions that support everything from array manipulation to regular expression support.

Database connectivity is one popular use for PHP. PHP supports a large number of databases natively and many others are accessible through PHP's ODBC functions.

Through this database connectivity, it is possible, for example, to take a company's database of products and write a web interface to it using PHP.

This book provides an overview of the core PHP language and contains summaries of all the functions available in PHP. The material covers PHP 3.0.

Installation and Configuration

PHP Version 3 can be installed in two primary ways: as an Apache module on Unix systems or as a CGI script on both Unix and Windows systems. See the installation instructions that come with PHP for full and current information.

When you are using PHP as an Apache module, PHP processing is triggered by a special MIME type. This is defined in the Apache configuration file with a line similar to:

```
AddType application/x-httpd-php3 .php3
```

This tells Apache to treat all files that end with the *.php3* extension as PHP files, which means that any file with that extension is parsed for PHP tags. The actual extension is completely arbitrary and you are free to change it to whatever you wish to use.

If you are running PHP as a dynamic shared object (DSO) module, you also need this line in your Apache configuration file:

```
LoadModule php3_module    modules/libphp3.so
```

When you are running PHP as a CGI script (with any web server), PHP processing is still triggered by this special MIME type, but a bit more work is needed. The web server needs to know that it has to redirect the request for the PHP MIME type to the CGI version of PHP. With

ApacheNT, for example, this redirect is done with a set of configuration lines like the following:

```
ScriptAlias /php3/ "/path-to-php-dir/php.exe"
AddType application/x-httpd-php3 .php3
Action application/x-httpd-php3 "/php3/php.exe"
```

For IIS, this redirect is set up through the Windows registry. Refer to the PHP installation instructions for full details.

At runtime, most aspects of PHP can be controlled with the *php3.ini* file (located in */usr/local/lib* by default). For the Apache module version of PHP, this file is read only when the server is started or reinitialized. Changes to this file should be treated the same as changes to Apache's own configuration files. In other words, if you make a change, you need to send your Apache server an HUB or a USR1 signal before the change will take effect.

Many aspects of PHP can also be controlled on a per-directory basis (or even per-location or per-request) when using the Apache module version. Most of the directives available in the *php3.ini* file are also available as native Apache directives. The name of a particular directive is the *php3.ini* name with "php3_" prepended. For a list of all available Apache directives, run your Apache *httpd* binary with the *–h* switch.

Embedding PHP in HTML

You embed PHP code into a standard HTML page. For example, here's how you can dynamically generate the title of an HTML document:

```
<HTML><HEAD><TITLE><?echo $title?></TITLE>
</HEAD>...
```

The <?echo $title?> portion of the document is replaced by the contents of the $title PHP variable. echo is a basic language statement that you can use to output data.

There are a few different ways that you can embed your PHP code. As you just saw, you can put PHP code between <? and ?> tags:

```
<? echo "Hello World"; ?>
```

This style is the most common way to embed PHP, but it is a problem if your PHP code needs to co-exist with XML, as XML may use that tagging style itself. If this is the case, you can turn off this style in the *php3.ini* file with the short_ open_tag directive. Another way to embed PHP code is within <?php and ?> tags:

```
<?php echo "Hello World"; ?>
```

This style is always available and is recommended when your PHP code needs to be portable to many different systems. Embedding PHP within <SCRIPT> tags is another style that is always available:

```
<SCRIPT LANGUAGE="php"> echo "Hello World";
</SCRIPT>
```

One final style, where the code is between <% and %> tags, is disabled by default:

```
<% echo "Hello World"; %>
```

You can turn on this style with the asp_tags directive in your *php3.ini* file. The style is most useful when you are using Microsoft FrontPage or another HTML authoring tool that prefers that tag style for HTML embedded scripts.

You can embed multiple statements by separating them with semicolons:

```
<?
echo "Hello World";
echo "A second statement";
?>
```

It is legal to switch back and forth between HTML and PHP at any time. For example, if you want to output 100 <BR> tags for some reason, you can do it this way:

```
<? for($i=0; $i<100; $i++) { ?>
<BR>
<? } ?>
```

When you embed PHP code in an HTML file, you need to use the *.php3* file extension for that file, so that your web server knows to send the file to PHP for processing. Or, if you have configured your web server to use a different extension for PHP files, use that extension instead.

When you have PHP code embedded in an HTML page, you can think of that page as being a PHP program. The bits and pieces of HTML and PHP combine to provide the functionality of the program. A collection of pages that contain programs can be thought of as a web application.

Including Files

An important feature of PHP is its ability to include files. These files may contain additional PHP tags. When you are designing a web application, it can be useful to break out some common components and place them in a single file. This makes it much easier to later change certain aspects in one place and have it take effect across the entire application. To include a file, you use the `include` keyword:

```
<?
$title="My Cool Web Application";
include "header.inc";
?>
```

The *header.inc* file might look as follows:

```
<HTML><HEAD>
<TITLE><?echo $title?></TITLE>
</HEAD>
```

This example illustrates two important concepts of included files in PHP. First, variables set in the including file are automatically available in the included file. Second, each included file starts out in HTML mode. In other words, if

---

you want to include a file that has PHP code in it, you have to embed that code just as you would any PHP code.

Language Syntax

Variable names in PHP are case-sensitive. That means that $A and $a are two distinct variables. However, function names in PHP are not case-sensitive. This applies to both built-in functions and user-defined functions.

PHP ignores whitespace between tokens. You can use spaces, tabs, and newlines to format and indent your code to make it more readable. PHP statements are terminated by semicolons.

There are three types of comments in PHP:

```
/* C style comments */
// C++ style comments
# Bourne shell style comments
```

The C++ and Bourne shell style comments can be inserted anywhere in your code. Everything from the comment characters to the end of the line is ignored. The C-style comment tells PHP to ignore everything from the start of the comment until the end-comment characters are seen. This means that this style of comment can span multiple lines.

Variables

In PHP, all variable names begin with a dollar sign ($). The $ is followed by an alphabetic character or an underscore, and optionally followed by a sequence of alphanumeric characters and underscores. There is no limit on the length of a variable. Variable names in PHP are case-sensitive. Here are some examples:

```
$i
$counter
$first_name
$_TMP
```

In PHP, unlike in many other languages, you do not have to explicitly declare variables. PHP automatically declares a variable the first time a value is assigned to it. PHP variables are untyped; you can assign a value of any type to a variable.

Dynamic Variables

Sometimes it is useful to set and use variables dynamically. Normally, you assign a variable like this:

```
$var = "hello";
```

Now let's say you want a variable whose name is the value of the $var variable. You can do that like this:

```
$$var = "World";
```

PHP parses $$var by first dereferencing the innermost variable, meaning that $var becomes "hello". The expression that is left is then $"hello", which is just $hello. In other words, we have just created a new variable named hello and assigned it the value "World". You can nest dynamic variables to an infinite level in PHP, although once you get beyond two levels, it can be very confusing for someone who is trying to read your code.

There is a special syntax for using dynamic variables inside quoted strings in PHP:

```
echo "Hello ${$var}";
```

This syntax is also used to help resolve an ambiguity that occurs when variable arrays are used. Something like $$var[1] is ambiguous because it is impossible for PHP to know which level to apply the array index to. ${$var[1]} tells PHP to dereference the inner level first and apply the array index to the result before dereferencing the outer level. ${$var}[1], on the other hand, tells PHP to apply the index to the outer level.

Dynamic variables may not initially seem that useful, but there are times when they can shorten the amount of code

---

you need to write to perform certain tasks. For example, say you have an associative array that looks like this:

```
$array["abc"] = "Hello";
$array["def"] = "World";
```

Associative arrays like this are returned by various functions in the PHP modules. mysql_fetch_array() is one example. The indices in the array usually refer to fields or entity names within the context of the module you are working with. It can be handy to turn these entity names into real PHP variables, so you can refer to them as simply $abc and $def. This can be done as follows:

```
while(list($index,$value) = each($array)) {
   $$index = $value;
}
```

Data Types

PHP provides three primitive data types: integers, floating point numbers, and strings. In addition, there are two compound data types: arrays and objects.

Integers

Integers are whole numbers. The range of integers in PHP is equivalent to the range of the long data type in C. On 32-bit platforms, integer values can range from –2,147,483,648 to +2,147,483,647. PHP automatically converts larger values to floating point numbers if you happen to overflow the range. An integer can be expressed in decimal (base-10), hexadecimal (base-16), or octal (base-8). For example:

```
$decimal=16;
$hex=0x10;
$octal=020;
```

Floating Point Numbers

Floating point numbers represent decimal values. The range of floating point numbers in PHP is equivalent to the range of the double type in C. On most platforms a double can range from 1.7E-308 to 1.7E+308. A double may be expressed either as a regular number with a decimal point or in scientific notation. For example:

```
$var=0.017;
$var=17.0E-3
```

Note that PHP also has a set of functions known as the BC (binary calculator) functions. These functions can manipulate arbitrary precision numbers. If you are dealing with very large numbers or numbers that require a high degree of precision, you should use these functions.

Strings

A string is a sequence of characters. A string can be delimited by single quotes or double quotes:

```
'PHP is cool'
"Hello, World!"
```

Double-quoted strings are subject to variable substitution and escape sequence handling, while single quotes are not. For example:

```
$a="World";
echo "Hello\t$a\n";
```

This displays "Hello" followed by a tab and then "World" followed by a newline. In other words, variable substitution is performed on the variable $a and the escape sequences are converted to their corresponding characters. Contrast that with:

```
echo 'Hello\t$a\n';
```

In this case, the output is exactly "Hello\t$a\n". There is no variable substitution or handling of escape sequences.

The following table shows the escape sequences under-stood by PHP:

Escape Sequence	Meaning
\n	Newline
\t	Tab
\r	Carriage return
\\	Backslash
\$	Dollar sign

Arrays

An array is a compound data type that can contain multi-ple data values, indexed either numerically or with strings. For example, an array of strings can be written like this:

```
$var[0]="Hello";
$var[1]="World";
```

Note that when you assign array elements like this, you do not have to use consecutive numbers to index the elements.

As a shortcut, PHP allows you to add an element onto the end of an array without specifying an index. For example:

```
$var[] ="Test";
```

PHP picks the next logical numerical index. In this case, the "Test" element is given the index 2 in our $var array: if the array has non-consecutive elements, PHP selects the index value that is one greater than the current highest index value. This auto-indexing feature is most useful when dealing with multiple-choice HTML <SELECT> form ele-ments, as we'll see in a later example.

Although we have called strings a primitive data type, it is actually possible to treat a string as a compound data type, where each character in the string can be accessed sepa-rately. In other words, you can think of a string as an array of characters, where the first character is at index 0. Thus, you can pick the third character out of a string with:

```
$string[2]
```

Arrays can also be indexed using strings; these kinds of arrays are called *associative arrays*:

```
$var["January"]=1;
$var["February"]=2;
```

In fact, you can use a mix of numerical and string indices with a single array. That is because internally PHP treats all arrays as hash tables and the hash, or index, can be whatever you want.

All arrays in PHP can be traversed safely with the following mechanism:

```
while(list($key,$value)=each($array)) {
  echo "array[$key]=$value<br>\n";
}
```

This is the most common way to loop through each element of an array, whether it is a linear or an associative array. PHP provides a number of array manipulation functions; these are detailed later in the "Function Reference" section.

Objects

An object is a compound data type that can contain any number of variables and functions. PHP's support for objects is very basic in Version 3. PHP Version 4 will improve the object-oriented capabilities of PHP. In PHP 3.0 the object-oriented support is designed to make it easy to encapsulate data structures and functions in order to package them into reusable classes. Here's a simple example:

```
class test {
  var $str = "Hello World";
  function init($str) {
    $this->str = $str;
```

```
    }
}

$class = new test;
print $class->str;
$class->init("Hello");
print $class->str;
```

This code creates a test object using the new operator. Then it sets a variable called str within the object. In object-speak, a variable in an object is known as a property of that object. The test object also defines a function, known as a method, called init( ). This method uses the special-purpose $this variable to change the value of the str property within that object.

If you are familiar with object-oriented programming, you should recognize that PHP's implementation is minimal. PHP3 does not support multiple inheritance, data protection (or encapsulation), and destructors. PHP does have inheritance and constructors, though.

Boolean Values

Every value in PHP has a boolean truth value (true or false) associated with it. This value is typically used in control structures, like if/else and for. The boolean value associated with a data value is determined as follows:

- For an integer or floating point value, the boolean value is false if the value is 0; otherwise the boolean value is true.

- For a string value, the boolean value is false if the string is empty; otherwise the boolean value is true.

- For an array, the boolean value is false if the array has no elements; otherwise the boolean value is true.

- For an object, the boolean value is false if the object has no defined variables or functions; otherwise the boolean value is true.

- For an undefined object (a variable that has not been defined at all), the boolean value is false.

PHP has two built-in keywords, true and false, where true represents the integer value 1 and false represents the empty string.

Type Casting

Variables in PHP do not need to be explicitly typed. PHP sets the type when a variable is first used in a script. You can explicitly specify a type using C-style casting.

For example:

```
$var = (int) "123abc";
```

Without the (int) in this example, PHP creates a string variable. With the explicit cast, however, we have created an integer variable with a value of 123. The following table shows the available cast operators in PHP:

Operators	Function
(int), (integer)	Cast to an integer
(real), (double), (float)	Cast to a floating point number
(string)	Cast to a string
(array)	Cast to an array
(object)	Cast to an object

Although they are not usually needed, PHP does provide the following built-in functions to check variable types in your program: gettype( ), is_long( ), is_double( ), is_string( ), is_array( ), and is_object( ).

Expressions

An expression is the basic building block of the language. Anything with a value can be thought of as an expression. Examples include:

```
5
5+5
$a
$a==5
sqrt(9)
```

By combining many of these basic expressions, you can build larger and more complex expressions.

Note that the `echo` statement we've used in numerous examples cannot be part of a complex expression because it does not have a return value. The `print` statement, on the other hand, can be used as part of complex expression, as it does have a return value. In all other respects, `echo` and `print` are identical—they output data.

Operators

Expressions are combined and manipulated using operators. The following table shows the operators available in PHP, along with their precedence (P) and associativity (A). The following table lists the operators from highest to lowest precedence. These operators should be familiar to you if you have any C, Java, or Perl experience.

Operators	P	A
!, ~, ++, --, @, (the casting operators)	16	Right
*, /, %	15	Left
+, - .	14	Left
<<, >>	13	Left
<, <=, >=, >	12	Non-associative
==, !=	11	Non-associative

Operators	P	A
&	10	Left
^	9	Left
|	8	Left
&&	7	Left
||	6	Left
? : (conditional operator)	5	Left
=, +=, -=, *=, /=, %=, ^=, .=, &=, |=	4	Left
And	3	Left
Xor	2	Left
Or	1	Left

Control Structures

The control structures in PHP are very similar to those used by the C language. Control structures are used to control the logical flow through a PHP script. PHP's control structures have two syntaxes that can be used interchangeably. The first form uses C-style curly braces to enclose statement blocks, while the second style uses a more verbose syntax that includes explicit ending statements. The first style is preferable when the control structure is completely within a PHP code block. The second style is useful when the construct spans a large section of intermixed code and HTML. The two styles are completely interchangeable, however, so it is really a matter of personal preference which one you use.

if

The if statement is a standard conditional found in most languages. Here are the two syntaxes for the if statement:

```
if(expr) {              if(expr):
  statements               statements
}                       elseif(expr):
```

```
elseif(expr) {              statements
  statements              else:
}                           statements
else {                    endif;
  statements
}
```

The if statement causes particular code to be executed if the expression it acts on is true. With the first form, you can omit the braces if you only need to execute a single statement.

switch

The switch statement can be used in place of a lengthy if statement. Here are the two syntaxes for switch:

```
switch(expr) {            switch(expr):
  case expr:                case expr:
    statements                statements
    break;                    break;
  default:                  default:
    statements                statements
    break;                    break;
}                         endswitch;
```

The expression for each case statement is compared against the switch expression and, if they match, the code following that particular case is executed. The break keyword signals the end of a particular case; it may be omitted, which causes control to flow into the next case. If none of the case expressions match the switch expression, the default case is executed.

while

The while statement is a looping construct that repeatedly executes some code while a particular expression is true:

```
while(expr) {             while(expr):
  statements                statements
}                         endwhile;
```

The `while` expression is checked before the start of each iteration. If the expression evaluates to `true`, the code within the loop is executed. If the expression evaluates to `false`, however, execution skips to the code immediately following the `while` loop. Note that you can omit the curly braces with the first form of the `while` statement if you only need to execute a single statement.

It is possible to break out of a running loop at any time using the `break` keyword. This stops the current loop and, if control is within a nested set of loops, the next outer loop continues. It is also possible to break out of many levels of nested loops by passing a numerical argument to the `break` statement (`break n`) that specifies the number of nested loops it should break out of. You can skip the rest of a given loop and go onto the next iteration by using the `continue` keyword. With `continue n`, you can skip the current iterations of the `n` innermost loops.

do/while

The `do/while` statement is similar to the `while` statement, except that the conditional expression is checked at the end of each iteration instead of before it:

```
do {
  statements
} while(expr);
```

Note that due to the order of the parts of this statement, there is only one valid syntax. If you only need to execute a single statement, you can omit the curly braces from the syntax. The `break` and `continue` statements work with this statement in the same way that they do with the `while` statement.

for

A `for` loop is a more complex looping construct than the simple `while` loop:

```
for(start_expr; cond_expr; iter_expr) {
  statements
}

for(start_expr; cond_expr; iter_expr):
  statements
endfor;
```

A for loop takes three expressions. The first is the start expression; it is evaluated once when the loop begins. This is generally used for initializing a loop counter. The second expression is a conditional expression that controls the iteration of the loop. This expression is checked prior to each iteration. The third expression, the iterative expression, is evaluated at the end of each iteration and is typically used to increment the loop counter. With the first form of the for statement, you can omit the braces if you only need to execute a single statement.

The break and continue statements work with a for loop like they do with a while loop, except that continue causes the iterative expression to be evaluated before the loop conditional expression is checked.

Functions

A function is a named sequence of code statements that can optionally accept parameters and return a value. A function call is an expression that has a value; its value is the returned value from the function. PHP provides a large number of internal functions. The "Function Reference" section lists all of the commonly available functions. PHP also supports user-definable functions. To define a function, use the function keyword. For example:

```
function soundcheck($a, $b, $c) {
  return "Testing, $a, $b, $c";
}
```

When you define a function, you need to be careful what name you give it. In particular, you need to make sure that

---

the name does not conflict with any of the internal PHP functions. If you do use a function name that conflicts with an internal function, you get the following error:

```
Fatal error: Can't redeclare already declared
function in filename on line N
```

After you define a function, you call it by passing in the appropriate arguments. For example:

```
echo soundcheck(4, 5, 6);
```

You can also create functions with optional parameters. To do so, you set a default value for each optional parameter in the definition, using C++ style. For example, here's how to make all the parameters to the soundcheck() function optional:

```
function soundcheck($a=1, $b=2, $c=3) {
 return "Testing, $a, $b, $c";
}
```

Variable Scope

The scope of a variable refers to where in a program the variable is available. If a variable is defined in the main part of a PHP script (i.e., not inside a function or a class), it is in the global scope. Note that global variables are only available during the current request. The only way to make variables in one page available to subsequent requests to another page is to pass them to that page via cookies, GET method data, or PUT method data. To access a global variable from inside a function, you need to use the global keyword. For example:

```
function test() {
 global $var;
 echo $var;
}
$var="Hello World";
test();
```

The $GLOBALS array is an alternative mechanism for accessing variables in the global scope. This is an associative array of all the variables currently defined in the global scope:

```php
function test() {
  echo $GLOBALS["var"];
}
$var="Hello World";
test();
```

Every function has its own scope. When you create a variable inside of a function, that variable has *local scope*. In other words, it is only available within the function. In addition, if there is a global variable with the same name as a variable within a function, any changes to the function variable do not affect the value of the global variable.

When you call a function, the arguments you pass to the function (if any) are defined as variables within the function, using the parameter names as variable names. Just as with variables created within a function, these passed arguments are only available within the scope of the function.

Passing Arguments

There are two ways you can pass arguments to a function: by value and by reference. To pass an argument by value, you pass in any valid expression. That expression is evaluated and the value is assigned to the corresponding parameter defined within the function. Any changes you make to the parameter within the function have no effect on the argument passed to the function. For example:

```php
function triple($x) {
  $x=$x*3;
  return $x;
}
$var=10;
$triplevar=triple($var);
```

In this case, $var evaluates to 10 when triple() is called, so $x is set to 10 inside the function. When $x is tripled, that change does not affect the value of $var outside the function.

In contrast, when you pass an argument by reference, changes to the parameter within the function do affect the value of the argument outside the scope of the function. That's because when you pass an argument by reference, you must pass a variable to the function. Now the parameter in the function refers directly to the value of the variable, meaning that any changes within the function are also visible outside the function. For example:

```
function triple($x) {
  $x=$x*3;
  return $x;
}
$var=10;
triple(&$var);
```

The & that precedes $var in the call to triple() causes the argument to be passed by reference, so the end result is that $var ends up with a value of 30.

Static Variables

PHP supports declaring local function variables as static. A static variable retains its value between function calls, but is still accessible only from within the function it is declared in. Static variables can be initialized and this initialization only takes place the first time the static declaration is executed. Static variables are often used as counters, as in this example:

```
function hitcount()
  static $count = 0;

  if ($count == 0) {
  print "This is the first time this page";
  print " has been accessed";
```

```
}
else {
 print "This page has been accessed $count";
 print  " times";
}
$count++;
}
```

Web-Related Variables

PHP automatically creates global variables for all the data it receives in an HTTP request. This can include GET data, POST data, cookie data, and environment variables. Say you have an HTML form that looks as follows:

```
<FORM ACTION="test.php3" METHOD="POST">
<INPUT TYPE=text NAME=var>
</FORM>
```

When the form is submitted to the *test.php3* file, the $var variable within that file is set to whatever the user entered in the text field.

A variable can also be set in a URL like this:

```
http://your.server/test.php3?var=Hello+World
```

When the request for this URL is processed, the $var variable is set for the *test.php3* page.

Any environment variables present in your web server's configuration are also made available, along with any CGI-style variables your web server might set. The actual set of variables varies between different web servers. The best way to get a list of these variables is to use PHP's special information tag. Put the following code in a page and load the page in your browser:

```
<? phpinfo() ?>
```

You should see a page with quite a bit of information about PHP and the machine it is running on. There is a table that describes each of the extensions currently enabled in PHP. Another table shows the current values of

---

all the various configuration directives from your *php3.ini* file. Following those two tables are more tables showing the regular environment variables, the special PHP internal variables, and the special environment variables that your web server has added. Finally, the HTTP request and response headers for the current request are shown.

Sometimes it is convenient to create a generic form handler, where you don't necessarily know all the form element names. To support this, PHP provides GET, POST, and cookie associative arrays that contain all of the data passed to the page using the different techniques. These arrays are named $HTTP_GET_DATA, $HTTP_POST_DATA, $HTTP_COOKIE_DATA, respectively. For example, here's another way to access the value of the text field in our form:

```
echo $HTTP_POST_VARS["var"];
```

PHP sets global variables in a particular order. By default, global variables are set first from GET data, then from POST data, and then finally from cookie data. This means that if you have a form with a field named var that uses the GET method and a cookie with a var value, there is just one global variable named $var that has the value of the cookie data. Of course, you can still get at the GET data through the $HTTP_GET_DATA array. The default order can be defined with the gpc_order directive in the *php3.ini* file.

Examples

The best way to understand the power of PHP is to examine some real examples of PHP in action, so we'll look at some common uses of PHP in this section.

Showing the Browser and IP Address

Here is a simple page that prints out the browser string and the IP address of the HTTP request. Create a file with the

following content in your web directory, name it something like *example.php3*, and load it in your browser:

```
<HTML><HEAD><TITLE>PHP Example</TITLE></HEAD>
<BODY>
You are using <? echo $HTTP_USER_AGENT ?><BR>
and coming from <? echo $REMOTE_ADDR ?>
</BODY></HTML>
```

You should see something like the following in your
browser window:

```
You are using Mozilla/4.0 (compatible; MSIE
4.01; Windows 98)
and coming from 207.164.141.23
```

Intelligent Form Handling

Here is a slightly more complex example. We are going to
create an HTML form that asks the user to enter a name
and select one or more interests from a selection box. We
could do this in two files, where we separate the actual
form from the data handling code, but instead, this example shows how it can be done in a single file:

```
<HTML><HEAD><TITLE>Form Example</TITLE></HEAD>
<BODY>
<H1>Form Example</H1>
<?
function show_form($first="", $last="",
                   $interest=""){
  $options = array("Sports", "Business",
                   "Travel", "Shopping",
                   "Computers");
  if(empty($interest)) $interest=array(-1);
?>
<FORM ACTION="form.php3" METHOD="POST">
First Name:
<INPUT TYPE=text NAME=first
        VALUE="<?echo $first?>">
<BR>
Last Name:
<INPUT TYPE=text NAME=last
```

```
         VALUE="<?echo $last?>">
<BR>
Interests:
<SELECT MULTIPLE NAME=interest[]>
<?
 for($i=0, reset($interest);
     $i<count($options); $i++){
   echo "<OPTION";
   if(current($interest)==$options[$i]) {
    echo " SELECTED ";
    next($interest);
    }
   echo "> $options[$i]\n";
  }
?>
</SELECT><BR>
<INPUT TYPE=submit>
</FORM>
<? }

if(!isset($first)) {
 show_form();
}
else {
 if(empty($first) || empty($last) ||
  count($interest) == 0) {
  echo "You did not fill in all the ";
  echo "fields, please try again<P>\n";
  show_form($first,$last,$interests);
 }
 else {
  echo "Thank you, $first $last, you ";
  echo "selected ". join(" and ", $interest);
  echo " as your interests.<P>\n";
 }
}
?>
</BODY></HTML>
```

There are a few things you should study carefully in this
example. First, we have isolated the display of the actual

---

form to a PHP function called show_form( ). This function is intelligent in that it can take the default value for each of the form elements as an optional argument. If the user does not fill in all the form elements, we use this feature to redisplay the form with whatever values the user has already entered. This means that the user only has to fill the fields he missed, which is much better than asking the user to hit the Back button or forcing him to reenter all the fields.

Notice how the file switches back and forth between PHP code and HTML. Right in the middle of defining our show_form( ) function, we switch back to HTML to avoid having numerous echo statements that just echo normal HTML. Then, when we need a PHP variable, we switch back to PHP code temporarily just to print the variable.

We've given the multiple-choice <SELECT> element the name interest[]. The [] on the name tells PHP that the data coming from this form element should be treated as an auto-indexed array. This means that PHP automatically gives each element the next sequential index, starting with 0 (assuming the array is empty to begin with).

The final thing to note is the way we determine what to display. We check if $first is set. If it isn't, we know that the user has not submitted the form yet, so we call show_form( ) without any arguments. This displays the empty form. If $first is set, however, we check to make sure that the $first and $last text fields are not empty and that the user has selected at least one interest.

Web Database Integration

To illustrate a complete database-driven application, we are going to build a little web application that lets people make suggestions and vote on what you should name your new baby. The example uses MySQL, but it can be changed to run on any of the databases that PHP supports.

The schema for our baby-name database looks like this:

```
CREATE TABLE baby_names (
 name varchar(30) NOT NULL,
 votes int(4),
 PRIMARY KEY (name)
);
```

This is in MySQL's query format and can be used directly to create the actual table. It simply defines a text field and an integer field. The text field is for the suggested baby name and the integer field is for the vote count associated with that name. We are making the name field a primary key, which means uniqueness is enforced, so that the same name cannot appear twice in the database.

We want this application to do a number of things. First, it should have a minimal check that prevents someone from voting many times in a row. We do this using a session cookie. Second, we want to show a fancy little barchart that depicts the relative share of the votes that each name has received. The barchart is created using a one pixel by one pixel blue dot GIF image and scaling the image using the height and width settings of the HTML <IMG> tag. We could also use PHP's built-in image functions to create a fancier looking bar.

Everything else is relatively straightforward form and database work. We use a couple of shortcuts as well. For example, instead of reading all the entries from the database and adding up all the votes in order to get a sum (which we need to calculate the percentages), we ask MySQL to do it for us with its built-in SUM function. The part of the code that displays all the names and their votes, along with the percentage bar, gets a little ugly, but you should be able to follow it. We are simply sending the correct HTML table tags before and after the various data we have fetched from the database.

Here's the full example:

```
<?
  if($vote && !$already_voted)
    SetCookie("already_voted","1");
?>
<HTML><HEAD><TITLE>Name the Baby</TITLE>
</HEAD><H3>Name the Baby</H3>
<FORM ACTION="baby.php3" METHOD="POST">
Suggestion: <INPUT TYPE=text NAME=new_name><P>
<INPUT TYPE=submit
       VALUE="Submit idea and/or vote">
<?
 mysql_pconnect("localhost","","");
 $db = "test";
 $table = "baby_names";

 if($new_name) {
  if(!mysql_db_query($db,
   "insert into $table values
   ('$new_name',0)")) {
    echo mysql_errno().": ";
    echo mysql_error()."<BR>";
  }
 }
 if($vote && $already_voted) {
  echo "<FONT COLOR=#ff0000>Hey, you voted ";
  echo "already! Vote ignored.</FONT><P>\n";
 }
 else if($vote) {
  if(!mysql_db_query($db,
   "update $table set votes=votes+1
   where name='$vote'")) {
   echo mysql_errno().": ";
   echo mysql_error()."<BR>";
  }
 }
 $result=mysql_db_query($db,
  "select sum(votes) as sum from $table");
 if($result) {
  $sum = (int) mysql_result($result,0,"sum");
  mysql_free_result($result);
```

```
    }

    $result=mysql_db_query($db,
      "select * from $table order by votes DESC");
    echo "<TABLE BORDER=0><TR><TH>Vote</TH>";
    echo "<TH>Idea</TH><TH COLSPAN=2>Votes</TH>";
    echo "</TR>\n";
    while($row=mysql_fetch_row($result)) {
     echo "<TR><TD ALIGN=center>";
     echo "<INPUT TYPE=radio NAME=vote ";
     echo "VALUE='$row[0]'></TD><TD>";
     echo $row[0]."</TD><TD ALIGN=right>";
     echo $row[1]."</TD><TD>";
     if($sum && (int)$row[1]) {
      $per = (int)(100 * $row[1]/$sum);
      echo "<IMG SRC=bline.gif HEIGHT=12 ";
      echo "WIDTH=$per> $per %</TD>";
     }
     echo "</TR>\n";
    }
    echo "</TABLE>\n";
    mysql_free_result($result);
    ?>
    <INPUT TYPE=submit
            VALUE="Submit idea and/or vote">
    <INPUT TYPE=reset>
    </FORM>
    </BODY></HTML>
```

Function Reference

The remaining sections summarize the internal functions
that are available in PHP. The synopsis for each function
lists the expected argument types for the function and its
return type. The possible types are int, double, string,
array, void, and mixed. mixed means that the argument
or return type can be of any type. Optional arguments are
shown in square brackets.

Array Functions

PHP supports arrays that are indexed both by integers and by arbitrary strings—known as associative arrays. Internally, PHP does not distinguish between associative arrays and integer-indexed arrays, as arrays are implemented as hash tables. Here are the array functions supported by PHP:

`array array(...)`
  Create an array that contains all of the specified arguments

`int array_walk(array array_arg, string function)`
  Apply a function to every member of an array

`int arsort(array array_arg)`
  Sort an array in reverse order and maintain index association

`int asort(array array_arg)`
  Sort an array and maintain index association

`int count(mixed var)`
  Count the number of elements in a variable (usually an array)

`mixed current(array array_arg)`
  Return the element currently pointed to by the internal array pointer

`array each(array array_arg)`
  Return the next key/value pair from an array

`mixed end(array array_arg)`
  Advance the array's internal pointer to the last element and return the value of that element

`void extract(array var_array, int extract_type [, string prefix])`
  Import variables into a symbol table from an array

`mixed key(array array_arg)`
  Return the key of the element currently pointed to by the internal array pointer

```
int krsort(array array_arg)
```
Sort an array in reverse by key

```
int ksort(array array_arg)
```
Sort an array by key

```
mixed max(mixed arg1 [, mixed arg2 [, ...]])
```
Return the highest value in an array or a series of arguments

```
mixed min(mixed arg1 [, mixed arg2 [, ...]])
```
Return the lowest value in an array or a series of arguments

```
mixed next(array array_arg)
```
Move the array's internal pointer to the next element and return the value of that element

```
mixed pos(array array_arg)
```
An alias for current( )

```
mixed prev(array array_arg)
```
Move the array's internal pointer to the previous element and return the value of that element

```
array range(int low, int high)
```
Create an array containing the range of integers from low to high (inclusive)

```
mixed reset(array array_arg)
```
Set the array's internal pointer to the first element and return the value of that element

```
int rsort(array array_arg)
```
Sort an array in reverse order

```
int shuffle(array array_arg)
```
Randomly shuffle the contents of an array

```
int sizeof(mixed var)
```
An alias for count( )

```
int sort(array array_arg)
```
Sort an array

```
int uasort(array array_arg, string cmp_function)
```
    Sort an array with a user-defined comparison function and maintain index association

```
int uksort(array array_arg, string cmp_function)
```
    Sort an array by keys using a user-defined comparison function

```
int usort(array array_arg, string cmp_function)
```
    Sort an array using a user-defined comparison function

Configuration and Logging Functions

Here are functions for getting and setting PHP configuration options at runtime, as well as logging and other functions that are useful during debugging:

```
int debugger_off(void)
```
    Disable the internal PHP debugger

```
int debugger_on(string ip_address)
```
    Enable the internal PHP debugger

```
int error_log(string message, int message_type [,
string destination] [, string extra_headers])
```
    Send an error message somewhere

```
int error_reporting([int level])
```
    Set/get the current error reporting level

```
string get_cfg_var(string option_name)
```
    Get the value of a PHP configuration option

```
int get_magic_quotes_gpc(void)
```
    Get the current active configuration setting of magic_quotes_gpc

```
int get_magic_quotes_runtime(void)
```
    Get the current active configuration setting of magic_quotes_runtime

---

```
void phpinfo(void)
```
Output a page of useful information about PHP and the current request

```
string phpversion(void)
```
Return the current PHP version

```
int set_magic_quotes_runtime(int new_setting)
```
Set the current active configuration setting of magic_quotes_runtime and return the previous value

```
void set_time_limit(int seconds)
```
Set the execution time limit for the current script

```
int short_tags(int state)
```
Turn the short tags option on or off and return the previous state

Syslog Functions

The syslog functions provide an interface to the Unix *syslog* facility. On NT, these functions have been abstracted to use NT's Event Log mechanism instead:

```
int closelog(void)
```
Close the connection to the system logger

```
void define_syslog_variables(void)
```
Initialize all *syslog*-related variables

```
int openlog(string ident, int option, int facility)
```
Open a connection to the system logger

```
int syslog(int priority, string message)
```
Generate a system log message

Database Functions

PHP supports a number of databases directly through the databases' own native APIs. Each of the databases is covered in a separate section. Many of the databases can also be accessed through ODBC if appropriate ODBC drivers

---

are available for that particular database. Adabas-D, Solid, Empress, Velocis and IBM DB2 have native APIs that are so similar to the ODBC API that having a separate set of functions for each one was redundant. So, for these five databases, use the ODBC set of functions. It is important to understand, however, that for those five databases, the actual communication is direct and native and does not go through any sort of intermediary ODBC layer.

dBase Functions

PHP allows you to access records stored in dBase-format (dbf) databases. dBase files are simple sequential files of fixed length records. Records are appended to the end of the file and deleted records are kept until you call `dbase_pack()`. Unlike with SQL databases, once a dBase file is created, the database definition is fixed. There are no indexes that speed searching or otherwise organize your data. Because of these limitations, I don't recommend using dBase files as your production database. Choose a real SQL server, such as MySQL or Postgres, instead. PHP provides dBase support to allow you to import and export data to and from your web database, as the format is understood by Windows spreadsheets and organizers. In other words, the import and export of data is about all that the dBase support is good for.

Here are the dBase functions supported by PHP:

`bool dbase_add_record(int identifier, array data)`
  Add a record to the database

`bool dbase_close(int identifier)`
  Close an open dBase-format database file

`bool dbase_create(string filename, array fields)`
  Create a new dBase-format database file

`bool dbase_delete_record(int identifier, int record)`
  Mark a record to be deleted

```
array dbase_get_record(int identifier, int
record)
```
Return an array representing a record from the database

```
array dbase_get_record_with_names(int identi-
fier, int record)
```
Return an associative array representing a record from
the database

```
int dbase_numfields(int identifier)
```
Return the number of fields (columns) in the database

```
int dbase_numrecords(int identifier)
```
Return the number of records in the database

```
int dbase_open(string name, int mode)
```
Open a dBase-format database file

```
bool dbase_pack(int identifier)
```
Pack the database (i.e., delete records marked for
deletion)

```
bool dbase_replace_record(int identifier, array
data, int recnum)
```
Replace a record to the database

DBA Functions

PHP supports DBM-style databases. This type of database
stores key/value pairs, as opposed to the full-blown records
supported by relational databases. As of PHP Version 3.0.8,
a DBM abstraction layer known as DBA has been added to
PHP, making it possible to access many different flavors of
DBM concurrently:

```
void dba_close(int handle)
```
Close a database

```
bool dba_delete(string key, int handle)
```
Delete the entry associated with key

```
bool dba_exists(string key, int handle)
```
Check if the specified key exists

```
string dba_fetch(string key, int handle)
```
Fetch the data associated with key

```
string dba_firstkey(int handle)
```
Reset the internal key pointer and return the first key

```
bool dba_insert(string key, string value, int
handle)
```
Insert value as key; returns false if key exists already

```
string dba_nextkey(int handle)
```
Return the next key

```
int dba_open(string path, string mode, string
handlername[, ...])
```
Open path using the specified handler in mode

```
bool dba_optimize(int handle)
```
Optimize (e.g., clean up, vacuum) database

```
int dba_popen(string path, string mode, string
handlername[, ...])
```
Open path using the specified handler in mode
persistently

```
bool dba_replace(string key, string value, int
handle)
```
Insert value as key; replaces key if key exists already

```
bool dba_sync(int handle)
```
Synchronize a database

DBM Functions

These are the older-style DBM functions that are likely to
be deprecated in a future version of PHP. The DBA functions should be used instead.

```
string dblist(void)
```
Describe the DBM-compatible library being used

```
bool dbmclose(int dbm_identifier)
```
Close a DBM database

```
int dbmdelete(int dbm_identifier, string key)
```
Delete the value for a key from a DBM database

```
int dbmexists(int dbm_identifier, string key)
```
Tell if a value exists for a key in a DBM database

```
string dbmfetch(int dbm_identifier, string key)
```
Fetch a value for a key from a DBM database

```
string dbmfirstkey(int dbm_identifier)
```
Retrieve the first key from a DBM database

```
int dbminsert(int dbm_identifier, string key,
string value)
```
Insert a value for a key in a DBM database

```
string dbmnextkey(int dbm_identifier, string key)
```
Retrieve the next key from a DBM database

```
int dbmopen(string filename, string mode)
```
Open a DBM database

```
int dbmreplace(int dbm_identifier, string key,
string value)
```
Replace the value for a key in a DBM database

Informix Functions

PHP supports Informix databases with the following functions:

```
int ifx_affected_rows(int resultid)
```
Return the number of rows affected by the query identified by resultid

```
void ifx_blobinfile_mode(int mode)
```
Set the default blob-mode for all select queries

```
void ifx_byteasvarchar(int mode)
```
Set the default byte-mode for all select queries

```
int ifx_close(int connid)
```
Close the Informix connection

```
int ifx_connect([string database[, string
userid[, string password]]])
```
Connect to the database using userid and password, if provided, and return a connection ID

```
int ifx_copy_blob(int bid)
```
Duplicate the given blob-object

```
int ifx_create_blob(int type, int mode, string
param)
```
Create a blob-object

```
int ifx_create_char(string param)
```
Create a char-object

```
int ifx_do(int resultid)
```
Execute a previously prepared query or open a cursor for it

```
string ifx_error( );
```
Return the Informix error codes (SQLSTATE and SQLCODE)

```
string ifx_errormsg([int errorcode])
```
Return the Informix error message associated with the error code

```
array ifx_fetch_row(int resultid, [mixed
position])
```
Fetch the next row or the position row if using a scroll cursor

```
array ifx_fieldproperties(int resultid)
```
Return an associative array for the resultid query, using field names as keys

```
array ifx_fieldtypes(int resultid)
```
Return an associative array with field names as keys for the query resultid

```
int ifx_free_blob(int bid)
```
Delete the blob-object

```
int ifx_free_char(int bid)
```
Delete the char-object

```
int ifx_free_result(int resultid)
```
Release resources for the query associated with resultid

```
string ifx_get_blob(int bid)
```
Return the content of the blob-object

```
string ifx_get_char(int bid)
```
Return the content of the char-object

```
int ifx_getsqlca(int $resultid)
```
Return the `sqlerrd[]` fields of the `sqlca` struct for query `$resultid`

```
int ifx_htmltbl_result(int resultid, [string
htmltableoptions])
```
Format all rows of the `resultid` query into an HTML table

```
void ifx_nullformat(int mode)
```
Set the default return value of a NULL value on a fetch-row

```
int ifx_num_fields(int resultid)
```
Return the number of columns in the query `resultid`

```
int ifx_num_rows(int resultid)
```
Return the number of rows already fetched for the query identified by `resultid`

```
int ifx_pconnect([string database[, string
userid[, string password]]])
```
Create a persistent connection to the database using `userid` and `password`, if specified, and return a connection ID

```
int ifx_prepare(string query, int connid, [int
cursortype], [array idarray])
```
Prepare a query on a given connection

```
int ifx_query(string query, int connid, [int
cursortype], [array idarray])
```
Perform a query on a given connection

```
void ifx_textasvarchar(int mode)
```
Set the default text-mode for all select queries

```
int ifx_update_blob(int bid, string content)
```
Update the content of the blob-object

```
int ifx_update_char(int bid, string content)
```
Update the content of the char-object

```
int ifxus_close_slob(int bid)
```
Delete the slob-object

```
int ifxus_create_slob(int mode)
```
Create a slob-object and open it

```
int ifxus_free_slob(int bid)
```
Delete the slob-object

```
int ifxus_open_slob(long bid, int mode)
```
Open a slob-object

```
int ifxus_read_slob(long bid, long nbytes)
```
Read nbytes of the slob-object

```
int ifxus_seek_slob(long bid, int mode, long
offset)
```
Set the current file or seek position of an open slob-object

```
int ifxus_tell_slob(long bid)
```
Return the current file or seek position of an open slob-object

```
int ifxus_write_slob(long bid, string content)
```
Write a string into the slob-object

mSQL Functions

PHP supports mSQL 1 and mSQL 2 databases with the following functions:

```
int msql_affected_rows(int query)
```
Return the number of affected rows

```
int msql_close([int link_identifier])
```
Close an mSQL connection

```
int msql_connect([string hostname[:port]] [,
string username] [, string password])
```
Open a connection to an mSQL server

```
int msql_create_db(string database_name [, int
link_identifier])
```
Create an mSQL database

```
int msql_data_seek(int query, int row_number)
```
Move the internal result pointer

```
int msql_db_query(string database_name, string
query [, int link_identifier])
```
Send an SQL query to mSQL

```
int msql_drop_db(string database_name [, int
link_identifier])
```
Drop (delete) an mSQL database

```
string msql_error([int link_identifier])
```
Return the text of the error message from the previous
mSQL operation

```
array msql_fetch_array(int query)
```
Fetch a result row as an associative array

```
object msql_fetch_field(int query [, int field_
offset])
```
Get column information from a result and return it as an
object

```
object msql_fetch_object(int query)
```
Fetch a result row as an object

```
array msql_fetch_row(int query)
```
Get a result row as an enumerated array

```
string msql_field_flags(int query, int field_
offset)
```
Get the flags associated with the specified field in a result

```
int msql_field_len(int query, int field_offet)
```
Return the length of the specified field

```
string msql_field_name(int query, int field_
index)
```
Get the name of the specified field in a result

```
int msql_field_seek(int query, int field_offset)
```
Set the result pointer to a specific field offset

```
string msql_field_table(int query, int field_
offset)
```
Get the name of the table the specified field is in

```
string msql_field_type(int query, int field_
offset)
```
Get the type of the specified field in a result

```
int msql_free_result(int query)
```
Free result memory

```
int msql_list_dbs([int link_identifier])
```
List databases available on an mSQL server

```
int msql_list_fields(string database_name, string
table_name [, int link_identifier])
```
List mSQL result fields

```
int msql_list_tables(string database_name [, int
link_identifier])
```
List tables in an mSQL database

```
int msql_num_fields(int query)
```
Get the number of fields in a result

```
int msql_num_rows(int query)
```
Get the number of rows in a result

```
int msql_pconnect([string hostname[:port]] [,
string username] [, string password])
```
Open a persistent connection to an mSQL server

```
int msql_query(string query [, int link_
identifier])
```
Send an SQL query to mSQL

```
int msql_result(int query, int row [, mixed
field])
```
Get result data

```
int msql_select_db(string database_name [, int
link_identifier])
```
Select an mSQL database

MySQL Functions

PHP supports MySQL 3.21.x, 3.22.x, and 3.23.x databases (*http://www.mysql.com/*) with the following functions:

```
int mysql_affected_rows([int link_identifier])
```
Get the number of affected rows in the previous MySQL operation

```
int mysql_change_user(string user, string pass-
word [, string database [, int link_
identifier]])
```
Change the logged-in user on the current connection

```
int mysql_close([int link_identifier])
```
Close a MySQL connection

```
int mysql_connect([string hostname[:port]] [,
string username] [, string password])
```
Open a connection to a MySQL server

```
int mysql_create_db(string database_name [, int
link_identifier])
```
Create a MySQL database

```
int mysql_data_seek(int result, int row_number)
```
Move the internal result pointer

```
int mysql_db_query(string database_name, string
query [, int link_identifier])
```
Send an SQL query to MySQL

```
int mysql_drop_db(string database_name [, int
link_identifier])
```
Drop (delete) a MySQL database

```
int mysql_errno([int link_identifier])
```
Return the number of the error message from the previous MySQL operation

```
string mysql_error([int link_identifier])
```
Return the text of the error message from the previous MySQL operation

```
array mysql_fetch_array(int result [, int result_
type])
```
Fetch a result row as an associative array

```
object mysql_fetch_field(int result [, int field_
offset])
```
Get column information from a result and return it as an object

```
array mysql_fetch_lengths(int result)
```
Get the maximum data size of each column in a result

```
object mysql_fetch_object(int result [, int
result_type])
```
Fetch a result row as an object

```
array mysql_fetch_row(int result)
```
Get a result row as an enumerated array

```
string mysql_field_flags(int result, int field_
offset)
```
Get the flags associated with the specified field in a result

```
int mysql_field_len(int result, int field_offet)
```
Return the length of the specified field

```
string mysql_field_name(int result, int field_
index)
```
Get the name of the specified field in a result

```
int mysql_field_seek(int result, int field_
offset)
```
Set the result pointer to a specific field offset

```
string mysql_field_table(int result, int field_
offset)
```
Get the name of the table the specified field is in

```
string mysql_field_type(int result, int field_
offset)
```
Get the type of the specified field in a result

```
int mysql_free_result(int result)
```
Free result memory

```
int mysql_insert_id([int link_identifier])
```
Get the ID generated from the previous INSERT operation

```
int mysql_list_dbs([int link_identifier])
```
List the databases available on a MySQL server

```
int mysql_list_fields(string database_name,
string table_name [, int link_identifier])
```
List MySQL result fields

```
int mysql_list_tables(string database_name [, int
link_identifier])
```
List the tables in a MySQL database

```
int mysql_num_fields(int result)
```
Get the number of fields in a result

```
int mysql_num_rows(int result)
```
Get the number of rows in a result

```
int mysql_pconnect([string hostname[:port][:/
path/to/socket]] [, string username] [, string
password])
```
Open a persistent connection to a MySQL server

```
int mysql_query(string query [, int link_
identifier])
```
   Send an SQL query to MySQL

```
int mysql_result(int result, int row [, mixed
field])
```
   Get result data

```
int mysql_select_db(string database_name [, int
link_identifier])
```
   Select a MySQL database

ODBC Functions

PHP supports ODBC databases with the following functions. Remember that these functions double as native API
functions for Adabas-D, Solid, Velocis, Empress, and IBM
DB2 databases.

```
int odbc_autocommit(int connection_id, int OnOff)
```
   Toggle autocommit mode

```
int odbc_binmode(int result_id, int mode)
```
   Handle binary column data

```
void odbc_close(int connection_id)
```
   Close an ODBC connection

```
void odbc_close_all(void)
```
   Close all ODBC connections

```
int odbc_commit(int connection_id)
```
   Commit an ODBC transaction

```
int odbc_connect(string DSN, string user, string
password [, int cursor_option])
```
   Connect to a data source

```
string odbc_cursor(int result_id)
```
   Get the cursor name

```
int odbc_exec(int connection_id, string query)
```
   Prepare and execute an SQL statement

```
int odbc_execute(int result_id [, array
parameters_array])
```
Execute a prepared statement

```
int odbc_fetch_into(int result_id [, int
rownumber], array result_array)
```
Fetch one result row into an array

```
int odbc_fetch_row(int result_id [, int row_
number])
```
Fetch a row

```
int odbc_field_len(int result_id, int field_
number)
```
Get the length of a column

```
string odbc_field_name(int result_id, int field_
number)
```
Get a column name

```
int odbc_field_num(int result_id, string field_
name)
```
Return the column number

```
string odbc_field_type(int result_id, int field_
number)
```
Get the data type of a column

```
int odbc_free_result(int result_id)
```
Free resources associated with a result

```
int odbc_longreadlen(int result_id, int length)
```
Handle LONG columns

```
int odbc_num_fields(int result_id)
```
Get the number of columns in a result

```
int odbc_num_rows(int result_id)
```
Get the number of rows in a result

```
int odbc_pconnect(string DSN, string user, string
password [, int cursor_option])
```
Establish a persistent connection to a data source

```
int odbc_prepare(int connection_id, string query)
```
Prepare a statement for execution

```
mixed odbc_result(int result_id, mixed field)
```
Get result data

```
int odbc_result_all(int result_id [, string
format])
```
Print results as an HTML table

```
int odbc_rollback(int connection_id)
```
Rollback a transaction

```
int odbc_setoption(int id, int function, int
option, int param)
```
Adjust ODBC settings

Oracle Functions

PHP supports Oracle 7.x and 8.x with the following
functions:

```
int ora_bind(int cursor, string php_variable_
name, string sql_parameter_name,int length [,
int type])
```
Bind a PHP variable to an Oracle parameter

```
int ora_close(int cursor)
```
Close an Oracle cursor

```
string ora_columnname(int cursor, int column)
```
Get the name of an Oracle result column

```
int ora_columnsize(int cursor, int column)
```
Return the size of the column

```
string ora_columntype(int cursor, int column)
```
Get the type of an Oracle result column

```
int ora_commit(int connection)
```
Commit an Oracle transaction

```
int ora_commitoff(int connection)
```
Disable automatic commit

```
int ora_commiton(int connection)
```
Enable automatic commit

```
int ora_do(int connection, int cursor)
```
Parse and execute a statement and fetch the first result row

```
string ora_error(int cursor_or_connection)
```
Get an Oracle error message

```
int ora_errorcode(int cursor_or_connection)
```
Get an Oracle error code

```
int ora_exec(int cursor)
```
Execute a parsed statement

```
int ora_fetch(int cursor)
```
Fetch a row of result data from a cursor

```
int ora_fetch_into(int cursor, array result)
```
Fetch a row into the specified result array

```
mixed ora_getcolumn(int cursor, int column)
```
Get data from a fetched row

```
int ora_logoff(int connection)
```
Close an Oracle connection

```
int ora_logon(string user, string password)
```
Open an Oracle connection

```
int ora_numcols(int cursor)
```
Return the numbers of columns in a result

```
int ora_numrows(int cursor)
```
Return the number of rows in a result

```
int ora_open(int connection)
```
Open an Oracle cursor

```
int ora_parse(int cursor, string sql_statement [,
int defer])
```
Parse an Oracle SQL statement

```
int ora_plogon(string user, string password)
```
Open a persistent Oracle connection

```
int ora_rollback(int connection)
```
   Roll back an Oracle transaction

Oracle OCI8 API

When linked against the new Oracle8 client libraries, the following functions can be used against any Oracle7 or Oracle8 server:

```
int OCIBindByName(int stmt, string name, mixed
&var, int maxlength [, int type])
```
   Bind a PHP variable to an Oracle placeholder by name

```
int OCICancel(int stmt)
```
   Prepare a new row of data for reading

```
int OCIColumnIsNULL(int stmt, int col)
```
   Tell whether a column is NULL

```
string OCIColumnName(int stmt, int col)
```
   Return the name of a column

```
int OCIColumnSize(int stmt, int col)
```
   Tell the maximum data size of a column

```
mixed OCIColumnType(int stmt, int col)
```
   Return the data type of a column

```
string OCICommit(int conn)
```
   Commit the current context

```
void OCIDebug(int onoff)
```
   Toggle internal debugging output for the OCI extension

```
int OCIDefineByName(int stmt, string name, mixed
&var [,int type])
```
   Define a PHP variable to an Oracle column by name

```
int OCIError([int stmt|conn])
```
   Return the last error of stmt|conn|global; if no error happened, returns false

```
int OCIExecute(int stmt [, int mode])
```
   Execute a parsed statement

```
int OCIFetch(int stmt)
```
Prepare a new row of data for reading

```
int OCIFetchInto(int stmt, array &output [, int
mode])
```
Fetch a row of result data into an array

```
int OCIFetchStatement(int stmt, array &output)
```
Fetch all rows of result data into an array

```
int OCIFreeStatement(int stmt)
```
Free all resources associated with a statement

```
int OCILogoff(int conn)
```
Disconnect from database

```
int OCILogon(string user, string pass[, string
db])
```
Connect to an Oracle database and log on

```
int OCINewCursor(int conn)
```
Allocate and return a new statement handle (cursor) for
the specified connection

```
string OCINewDescriptor(int connection [,int type
])
```
Initialize a new empty descriptor LOB/FILE (LOB is
default)

```
int OCINLogon(string user, string pass[, string
db])
```
Connect to an Oracle database and log on

```
int OCINumCols(int stmt)
```
Return the number of result columns in a statement

```
int OCIParse(int conn, string query)
```
Parse a query and return a statement

```
int OCIPLogon(string user, string pass[, string
db])
```
Connect to an Oracle database and log on using a persistent connection

---

```
string OCIResult(int stmt, mixed column)
```
Return a single column of result data

```
string OCIRollback(int conn)
```
Rollback the current context

```
string OCIServerVersion(int conn)
```
Return a string the contains server version information

```
int OCIStatementType(int stmt)
```
Return the query type of an OCI statement

PostgreSQL Functions

PostgreSQL is an open source database available at *http://www.postgreSQL.org*. PHP supports PostgreSQL databases with the following functions:

```
bool pg_close([int connection])
```
Close a PostgreSQL connection

```
int pg_cmdtuples(int result)
```
Return the number of affected tuples

```
int pg_connect([string connection_string] |
[string host, string port, [string options,
[string tty,]] string database)
```
Open a PostgreSQL connection

```
string pg_dbname([int connection])
```
Get the database name

```
string pg_errormessage([int connection])
```
Get the error message string

```
int pg_exec([int connection,] string query)
```
Execute a query

```
array pg_fetch_array(int result, int row)
```
Fetch a row as an array

```
object pg_fetch_object(int result, int row)
```
Fetch a row as an object

```
array pg_fetch_row(int result, int row)
```
Get a row as an enumerated array

```
int pg_fieldisnull(int result, int row, mixed
field_name_or_number)
```
Test if a field is NULL

```
string pg_fieldname(int result, int field_
number)
```
Return the name of the field

```
int pg_fieldnum(int result, string field_name)
```
Return the field number of the named field

```
int pg_fieldprtlen(int result, int row, mixed
field_name_or_number)
```
Return the printed length

```
int pg_fieldsize(int result, int field_number)
```
Return the internal size of the field

```
string pg_fieldtype(int result, int field_
number)
```
Return the type name for the given field

```
int pg_freeresult(int result)
```
Free result memory

```
int pg_getlastoid(int result)
```
Return the last object identifier

```
string pg_host([int connection])
```
Return the host name associated with the connection

```
void pg_loclose(int fd)
```
Close a large object

```
int pg_locreate(int connection)
```
Create a large object

```
int pg_loopen([int connection,] int objoid,
string mode)
```
Open a large object and return the file descriptor

```
string pg_loread(int fd, int len)
```
Read a large object

```
void pg_loreadall(int fd)
```
Read a large object and send it straight to the browser

```
void pg_lounlink([int connection, ] int large_
obj_id)
```
Delete a large object

```
int pg_lowrite(int fd, string buf)
```
Write a large object

```
int pg_numfields(int result)
```
Return the number of fields in the result

```
int pg_numrows(int result)
```
Return the number of rows in the result

```
string pg_options([int connection])
```
Get the options associated with the connection

```
int pg_pconnect([string connection_string] |
[string host, string port, [string options,
[string tty,]] string database)
```
Open a persistent PostgreSQL connection

```
int pg_port([int connection])
```
Return the port number associated with the connection

```
mixed pg_result(int result, int row_number, mixed
field_name)
```
Return values from a result identifier

```
string pg_tty([int connection])
```
Return the tty name associated with the connection

Sybase Functions

PHP supports Sybase databases with the following
functions:

```
int sybase_affected_rows([int link_id])
```
Get the number of affected rows in the last query

```
bool sybase_close([int link_id])
```
   Close a Sybase connection

```
int sybase_connect([string host[, string user[,
string password]]])
```
   Open a Sybase server connection

```
bool sybase_data_seek(int result, int offset)
```
   Move the internal row pointer

```
array sybase_fetch_array(int result)
```
   Fetch a row as an array

```
object sybase_fetch_field(int result[, int
offset])
```
   Get field information

```
object sybase_fetch_object(int result)
```
   Fetch a row as an object

```
array sybase_fetch_row(int result)
```
   Get a row as an enumerated array

```
bool sybase_field_seek(int result, int offset)
```
   Set the field offset

```
bool sybase_free_result(int result)
```
   Free result memory

```
string sybase_get_last_message(void)
```
   Return the last message from the server

```
int sybase_num_fields(int result)
```
   Get the number of fields in result

```
int sybase_num_rows(int result)
```
   Get the number of rows in result

```
int sybase_pconnect([string host[, string user[,
string password]]])
```
   Open a persistent Sybase connection

```
int sybase_query(string query[, int link_id])
```
   Send a Sybase query

```
string sybase_result(int result, int row, mixed
field)
```
    Get result data

```
bool sybase_select_db(string database[, int link_
id])
```
    Select a Sybase database

Date/Time Functions

PHP provides the following functions for working with dates and times:

```
bool checkdate(int month, int day, int year)
```
    Validate a date/time

```
string date(string format[, int timestamp])
```
    Format a local date/time

```
array getdate([int timestamp])
```
    Get date/time information

```
array gettimeofday(void)
```
    Return the current time as an array

```
string gmdate(string format[, int timestamp])
```
    Format a GMT/CUT date/time

```
int gmmktime(int hour, int min, int sec, int mon,
int mday, int year)
```
    Get Unix timestamp for a GMT date

```
string gmstrftime(string format[, int timestamp])
```
    Format a GMT/CUT time/date according to local settings

```
string microtime(void)
```
    Return a string containing the current time in seconds and microseconds

```
int mktime(int hour, int min, int sec, int mon,
int mday, int year)
```
    Get Unix timestamp for a date

```
string strftime(string format[, int timestamp])
```
Format a local time/date according to local settings

```
int time(void)
```
Return current Unix timestamp

Directory Functions

The following functions are used to manipulate directories. For example, to open the current directory and read in all the entries, you can do something like this:

```
$handle = opendir('.');
while($entry = readdir($handle)) {
    echo "$entry<br>\n";
}
closedir($handle);
```

PHP supports a dir class that represents a directory. Here's an example of using this object-oriented approach to reading a directory:

```
$d = dir("/etc");
echo "Handle: ".$d->handle."<br>\n";
echo "Path: ".$d->path."<br>\n";
while($entry=$d->read()) {
    echo $entry."<br>\n";
}
$d->close();
```

In addition to the read() and close() methods, the dir class supports a rewind() method.

Here are the directory functions supported by PHP:

```
int chdir(string directory)
```
Change the current directory

```
void closedir([int dir_handle])
```
Close the directory connection identified by the dir_handle, or a previously opened directory if not specified

---

```
class dir(string directory)
```
Return a class with handle and path properties as well as read, rewind, and close methods

```
int opendir(string directory)
```
Open a directory and return a dir_handle

```
string readdir(int dir_handle)
```
Read a directory entry from dir_handle

```
void rewinddir(int dir_handle)
```
Rewind dir_handle back to the start

File Functions

The following functions manipulate the local filesystem or data from the filesystem in some manner:

```
string basename(string path)
```
Return the filename component of the path

```
int chgrp(string filename, mixed group)
```
Change the file group

```
int chmod(string filename, int mode)
```
Change the file mode

```
int chown(string filename, mixed user)
```
Change the file owner

```
void clearstatcache(void)
```
Clear the file stat cache

```
int copy(string source_file, string destination_
file)
```
Copy a file

```
string dirname(string path)
```
Return the directory name component of the path

```
bool diskfree(string path)
```
Return the number of free kilobytes in path

```
int fclose(int fp)
```
Close an open file pointer

```
int feof(int fp)
```
Test for end-of-file on a file pointer

```
string fgetc(int fp)
```
Get a character from the file pointer

```
array fgetcsv(int fp, int length)
```
Get line from file pointer and parse for CSV fields

```
string fgets(int fp, int length)
```
Get a line from the file pointer

```
string fgetss(int fp, int length [, string
allowable_tags])
```
Get a line from the file pointer and strip HTML tags

```
array file(string filename [, int use_include_
path])
```
Read an entire file into an array

```
int file_exists(string filename)
```
Check whether a file exists or not

```
int fileatime(string filename)
```
Get the last access time for a file

```
int filectime(string filename)
```
Get the last inode status change for a file

```
int filegroup(string filename)
```
Return the group ID of the file

```
int fileinode(string filename)
```
Return the inode number of the file

```
int filemtime(string filename)
```
Return the time the file was last modified

```
int fileowner(string filename)
```
Return the user ID of the owner of the file

```
int fileperms(string filename)
```
Return the file permission bits of the file

```
int filesize(string filename)
```
Return the size of the file

```
string filetype(string filename)
```
Return the type of the file (fifo, char, block, link, file, or unknown)

```
bool flock(int fp, int operation)
```
Place or remove an advisory lock on a file

```
int fopen(string filename, string mode [, int use_include_path])
```
Open a file or a URL and return a file pointer

```
int fpassthru(int fp)
```
Output all remaining data from a file pointer

```
int fputs(int fp, string str [, int length])
```
Write to a file pointer

```
int fread(int fp, int length)
```
Binary-safe file read

```
int fseek(int fp, int offset)
```
Seek on a file pointer

```
int ftell(int fp)
```
Get the file pointer's read/write position

```
int fwrite(int fp, string str [, int length])
```
Binary-safe file write

```
array get_meta_tags(string filename [, int use_include_path])
```
Extract all meta tag content attributes from a file and return an array

```
bool is_dir(string pathname)
```
Returns true if the pathname is a directory

```
bool is_executable(string filename)
```
Return true if filename is executable

```
bool is_file(string filename)
```
Return true if filename is a regular file

```
bool is_link(string filename)
```
Return true if filename is a symbolic link

```
bool is_readable(string filename)
```
Return true if filename exists and is readable

```
bool is_writeable(string filename)
```
Return true if filename exists and is writeable

```
int link(string target, string link)
```
Create a hard link

```
int linkinfo(string filename)
```
Return the st_dev field of the Unix C stat structure describing the link

```
array lstat(string filename)
```
Return an array that contains information about the file; follows symbolic links

```
int mkdir(string pathname, int mode)
```
Create a directory

```
int pclose(int fp)
```
Close a file pointer opened by popen( )

```
int popen(string command, string mode)
```
Execute a command and open either a read or a write pipe to it

```
int readfile(string filename)
```
Output a file or a URL

```
int readlink(string filename)
```
Return the target of a symbolic link

```
int rename(string old_name, string new_name)
```
Rename a file

```
int rewind(int fp)
```
Rewind the position of a file pointer

```
int rmdir(string dirname)
```
Remove a directory

```
int set_file_buffer(int fp, int buffer)
```
Set file write buffer

```
array stat(string filename)
```
Return an array that contains information about the file; does not follow symbolic links

```
int symlink(string target, string link)
```
Create a symbolic link

```
string tempnam(string dir, string prefix)
```
Create a unique filename in a directory

```
int touch(string filename[, int time])
```
Create an empty file, or set modification time of an existing one

```
int umask(int mask)
```
Change the current umask

```
int unlink(string filename)
```
Delete a file

GZIP File Functions

These functions are used to transparently manipulate files that have been placed in a GZIP archive:

```
int gzclose(int zp)
```
Close an open GZIP file pointer

```
int gzeof(int zp)
```
Test for end-of-file on a GZIP file pointer

```
array gzfile(string filename [, int use_include_path])
```
Read and uncompress an entire GZIP file into an array

```
string gzgetc(int zp)
```
Get a character from a GZIP file pointer

```
string gzgets(int zp, int length)
```
Get a line from a GZIP file pointer

```
string gzgetss(int zp, int length, [string allowable_tags])
```
Get a line from a GZIP file pointer and strip HTML tags

```
int gzopen(string filename, string mode [, int
use_include_path])
```
Open a GZIP file and return a GZIP file pointer

```
int gzpassthru(int zp)
```
Output all remaining data from a GZIP file pointer

```
int gzputs(int zp, string str [, int length])
```
An alias for gzwrite()

```
int gzread(int zp, int length)
```
Binary-safe GZIP file read

```
int gzrewind(int zp)
```
Rewind the position of a GZIP file pointer

```
int gzseek(int zp, int offset)
```
Seek on a GZIP file pointer

```
int gztell(int zp)
```
Get a GZIP file pointer's read/write position

```
int gzwrite(int zp, string str [, int length])
```
Binary-safe GZIP file write

```
int readgzfile(string filename [, int use_
include_path])
```
Output a GZIP file

Graphics Functions

The graphics functions in PHP can be used to dynamically create a GIF image stream. This stream can either be sent directly to the browser or saved in a standard GIF file. The following example illustrates a number of these image functions:

```
Header("Content-type: image/gif");
if(!isset($s)) $s=11;
$size = imagettfbbox($s,0,
  "/fonts/TIMES.TTF",$text);
$dx = abs($size[2]-$size[0]);
$dy = abs($size[5]-$size[3]);
$xpad=9; $ypad=9;
```

```
$im = imagecreate($dx+$xpad,$dy+$ypad);
$blue = ImageColorAllocate($im,0x2c,0x6D,
   0xAF);
$black = ImageColorAllocate($im,0,0,0);
$white = ImageColorAllocate($im,255,255,255);
ImageRectangle($im,0,0,$dx+$xpad-1,
   $dy+$ypad-1, $black);
ImageRectangle($im,0,0,$dx+$xpad,$dy+$ypad,
   $white);
ImageTTFText($im, $s, 0, (int)($xpad/2)+1,
   $dy+(int)($ypad/2), $black,
   "/fonts/TIMES.TTF", $text);
ImageTTFText($im, $s, 0, (int)($xpad/2),
   $dy+(int)($ypad/2)-1, $white,
   "/fonts/TIMES.TTF", $text);
ImageGif($im);
ImageDestroy($im);
```

This example should be saved as a file named *button.php3*,
for example, and then called as part of an HTML <IMG> tag
like this:

```
<IMG SRC="button.php3?s=13&text=Help">.
```

This produces a blue-shaded button with white shadowed
text using a 13-point Times font.

Because of Unisys patent issues, the GD library (as of version 1.6) that PHP links against to generate GIF images no
longer supports the GIF format. Older versions of the GD
library will continue to work fine with PHP, and as of PHP-
3.0.13 you can use the later versions of GD to create images in the PNG format. In the above example, you simply
change the ImageGif($im) call to ImagePng($im).

Here are the graphics functions provided by PHP:

```
array getimagesize(string filename [, array
info])
```
   Get the size of a GIF, JPG, or PNG image as a four-
   element array

```
int imagearc(int im, int cx, int cy, int w, int
h, int s, int e, int col)
```
Draw a partial ellipse

```
int imagechar(int im, int font, int x, int y,
string c, int col)
```
Draw a character

```
int imagecharup(int im, int font, int x, int y,
string c, int col)
```
Draw a character rotated 90 degrees counter-clockwise

```
int imagecolorallocate(int im, int red, int
green, int blue)
```
Allocate a color for an image

```
int imagecolorat(int im, int x, int y)
```
Get the index of the color of a pixel

```
int imagecolorclosest(int im, int red, int green,
int blue)
```
Get the index of the closest color to the specified color

```
int imagecolordeallocate(int im, int index)
```
Deallocate a color for an image

```
int imagecolorexact(int im, int red, int green,
int blue)
```
Get the index of the specified color

```
int imagecolorresolve(int im, int red, int green,
int blue)
```
Get the index of the specified color or its closest possible alternative

```
int imagecolorset(int im, int col, int red, int
green, int blue)
```
Set the color for the specified palette index

```
array imagecolorsforindex(int im, int col)
```
Get the colors for an index

```
int imagecolorstotal(int im)
```
Find out the number of colors in an image's palette

```
int imagecolortransparent(int im [, int col])
```
Define a color as transparent

```
int imagecopy(int dst_im, int src_im, int dstX,
int dstY, int srcX, int srcY, int srcW, int
srcH)
```
Copy part of an image

```
int imagecopyresized(int dst_im, int src_im, int
dstX, int dstY, int srcX, int srcY, int dstW,
int dstH, int srcW, int srcH);
```
Copy and resize part of an image

```
int imagecreate(int x_size, int y_size)
```
Create a new image

```
int imagecreatefromgif(string filename)
```
Create a new image from a GIF file or URL

```
int imagecreatefrompng(string filename)
```
Create a new image from a PNG file or URL

```
int imagedashedline(int im, int x1, int y1, int
x2, int y2, int col)
```
Draw a dashed line

```
int imagedestroy(int im)
```
Destroy an image

```
int imagefill(int im, int x, int y, int col)
```
Flood-fill

```
int imagefilledpolygon(int im, array point, int
num_points, int col)
```
Draw a filled polygon

```
int imagefilledrectangle(int im, int x1, int y1,
int x2, int y2, int col)
```
Draw a filled rectangle

```
int imagefilltoborder(int im, int x, int y, int
border, int col)
```
Flood-fill to specific color

```
int imagefontheight(int font)
```
   Get the font height

```
int imagefontwidth(int font)
```
   Get the font width

```
int imagegammacorrect(int im, double input-
gamma, double outputgamma)
```
   Apply a gamma correction to an image

```
int imagegif(int im [, string filename])
```
   Output a GIF image to browser or file

```
int imageinterlace(int im [, int interlace])
```
   Enable or disable interlacing

```
int imageline(int im, int x1, int y1, int x2, int
y2, int col)
```
   Draw a line

```
int imageloadfont(string filename)
```
   Load a new font

```
int imagepng(int im [, string filename])
```
   Output a PNG image to browser or file

```
int imagepolygon(int im, array point, int num_
points, int col)
```
   Draw a polygon

```
array imagepsbbox(string text, int font, int
size[, int space, int tightness, int angle])
```
   Return the bounding box needed by a PostScript Type-1
   font string if rasterized

```
bool imagepsencodefont(int font_index, string
filename)
```
   Change the character encoding vector of a PostScript
   Type-1 font

```
bool imagepsextendfont(int font_index, double
extend)
```
   Extend or condense (if extend greater than 1) a Post-
   Script Type-1 font

```
bool imagepsfreefont(int font_index)
```
Free memory used by a PostScript Type-1 font

```
int imagepsloadfont(string pathname)
```
Load a new PostScript Type-1 font from specified file

```
bool imagepsslantfont(int font_index, double
slant)
```
Slant a PostScript Type-1 font

```
array imagepstext(int image, string text, int
font, int size, int xcoord, int ycoord [, int
space, int tightness, double angle, int
antialias])
```
Rasterize a PostScript Type-1 font string over an image

```
int imagerectangle(int im, int x1, int y1, int
x2, int y2, int col)
```
Draw a rectangle

```
int imagesetpixel(int im, int x, int y, int col)
```
Set a single pixel

```
int imagestring(int im, int font, int x, int y,
string str, int col)
```
Draw a string horizontally

```
int imagestringup(int im, int font, int x, int y,
string str, int col)
```
Draw a string vertically (i.e., rotated 90 degrees counter-clockwise)

```
int imagesx(int im)
```
Get the image width

```
int imagesy(int im)
```
Get the image height

```
array imagettfbbox(int size, int angle, string
font_file, string text)
```
Give the bounding box of some text using TrueType fonts

```
array imagettftext(int im, int size, int angle,
int x, int y, int col, string font_file, string
text)
```
Write text to the image using a TrueType font

```
array iptcembed(string iptcdata, string jpeg_
file_name [ , int spool ])
```
Embed binary IPTC data into a JPEG image.

```
array iptcparse(string jpeg_image)
```
Read the IPTC header from a JPEG image file

HTTP Functions

These functions assist you in dealing with the HTTP proto-col. The encoding and decoding functions are not normally needed, as PHP takes care of these actions automatically. But there are cases where the actions need to be done manually, so these functions are provided. The header and cookie functions are useful for either sending custom HTTP headers or sending cookies.

Here are the HTTP functions in PHP:

```
int header(string str)
```
Send a raw HTTP header

```
int headers_sent(void)
```
Return true if headers have already been sent, false otherwise

```
array parse_url(string url)
```
Parse a URL and return its components in an array

```
string rawurldecode(string str)
```
Decode a URL-encoded string

```
string rawurlencode(string str)
```
URL-encode a string

```
void setcookie(string name [, string value [, int
expire [, string path [, string domain [, int
secure ]]]]])
```
   Send a cookie

```
string urldecode(string str)
```
   Decode a URL-encoded string

```
string urlencode(string str)
```
   URL-encode a string

Apache-Specific Functions

The following HTTP functions are only available if PHP is
running as an Apache module:

```
class apache_lookup_uri(string URI)
```
   Perform a partial request of the given URI to obtain
   information about it

```
string apache_note(string note_name [, string
note_value])
```
   Get and set Apache request notes

```
array getallheaders(void)
```
   Fetch all HTTP request headers

```
int virtual(string filename)
```
   Perform an Apache subrequest

IMAP Functions

These functions are used to communicate with mail and
news servers via the IMAP4, POP3, or NNTP protocols. For
these functions to work, you have to compile PHP with
-- with-imap. That requires the C-client library to be
installed. You can get the latest version from *ftp://*
ftp.cac.washington.edu/imap/.

Here are the IMAP functions:

```
string imap_8bit(string text)
```
   Convert an 8-bit string to a quoted-printable string

```
string imap_alerts(void)
```
Return an array of all IMAP alerts

```
int imap_append(int stream_id, string folder,
string message [, string flags])
```
Append a string message to a specified mailbox

```
string imap_base64(string text)
```
Decode base64-encoded text

```
string imap_binary(string text)
```
Convert an 8-bit string to a base64-encoded string

```
string imap_body(int stream_id, int msg_no [, int
options])
```
Read the message body

```
object imap_bodystruct(int stream_id, int msg_
no, int section)
```
Read the structure of a specified body section of a specific message

```
object imap_check(int stream_id)
```
Get mailbox properties

```
void imap_clearflag_full(int stream_id, string
sequence, string flag [, int options])
```
Clear flags on messages

```
int imap_close(int stream_id [, int options])
```
Close an IMAP stream

```
int imap_create(int stream_id, string mailbox)
```
An alias for imap_createmailbox()

```
int imap_createmailbox(int stream_id, string
mailbox)
```
Create a new mailbox

```
int imap_delete(int stream_id, int msg_no)
```
Mark a message for deletion

```
bool imap_deletemailbox(int stream_id, string
mailbox)
```
Delete a mailbox

```
string imap_errors(void)
```
Return an array of all IMAP errors

```
int imap_expunge(int stream_id)
```
Delete all messages marked for deletion

```
array imap_fetch_overview(int stream_id, int msg_
no)
```
Read an overview of the information in the headers of
the given message

```
string imap_fetchbody(int stream_id, int msg_no,
int section [, int options])
```
Get a specific body section

```
string imap_fetchheader(int stream_id, int msg_
no [, int options])
```
Get the full, unfiltered header for a message

```
object imap_fetchstructure(int stream_id, int
msg_no [, int options])
```
Read the full structure of a message

```
string imap_fetchtext(int stream_id, int msg_no
[, int options])
```
An alias for imap_body()

```
array imap_getmailboxes(int stream_id, string
ref, string pattern)
```
Read the list of mailboxes and return a full array of
objects containing name, attributes, and delimiter

```
array imap_getsubscribed(int stream_id, string
ref, string pattern)
```
Return a list of subscribed mailboxes

```
object imap_header(int stream_id, int msg_no [,
int from_length [, int subject_length [, string
default_host]]])
```
Read the header of the message

```
object imap_headerinfo(int stream_id, int msg_no
[, int from_length [, int subject_length [,
string default_host]]])
```
An alias for imap_header( )

```
array imap_headers(int stream_id)
```
Return headers for all messages in a mailbox

```
string imap_last_error(void)
```
Return the last error generated by an IMAP function

```
array imap_list(int stream_id, string ref, string
pattern)
```
Read the list of mailboxes

```
array imap_listmailbox(int stream_id, string ref,
string pattern)
```
An alias for imap_list( )

```
array imap_listsubscribed(int stream_id, string
ref, string pattern)
```
An alias for imap_lsub( )

```
array imap_lsub(int stream_id, string ref, string
pattern)
```
Return a list of subscribed mailboxes

```
string imap_mail_compose(array envelope, array
body)
```
Create a MIME message based on given envelope and
body sections

```
int imap_mail_copy(int stream_id, int msg_no,
string mailbox [, int options])
```
Copy specified message to a mailbox

```
bool imap_mail_move(int stream_id, int msg_no,
string mailbox)
```
Move specified message to a mailbox

```
array imap_mailboxmsginfo(int stream_id)
```
Return information about the current mailbox in an associative array

---

```
int imap_msgno(int stream_id, int unique_msg_id)
```
Get the sequence number associated with a UID

```
int imap_num_msg(int stream_id)
```
Give the number of messages in the current mailbox

```
int imap_num_recent(int stream_id)
```
Give the number of recent messages in current mailbox

```
int imap_open(string mailbox, string user, string
password [, int options])
```
Open an IMAP stream to a mailbox

```
int imap_ping(int stream_id)
```
Check if the IMAP stream is still active

```
int imap_popen(string mailbox, string user,
string password [, int options])
```
Open an IMAP stream to a mailbox

```
string imap_qprint(string text)
```
Convert a quoted-printable string to an 8-bit string

```
int imap_rename(int stream_id, string old_name,
string new_name)
```
An alias for imap_renamemailbox( )

```
int imap_renamemailbox(int stream_id, string old_
name, string new_name)
```
Rename a mailbox

```
int imap_reopen(int stream_id, string mailbox [,
int options])
```
Reopen IMAP stream to new mailbox

```
array imap_rfc822_parse_adrlist(string address_
string, string default_host)
```
Parse an address string

```
string imap_rfc822_write_address(string mailbox,
string host, string personal)
```
Return a properly formatted email address given the
mailbox, host, and personal info

```
array imap_scan(int stream_id, string ref, string
pattern, string content)
```
   Read list of mailboxes containing a certain string

```
array imap_scanmailbox(int stream_id, string ref,
string pattern, string content)
```
   An alias for imap_scan( )

```
array imap_search(int stream_id, string criteria
[, long flags])
```
   Return a list of messages matching the criteria

```
int imap_setflag_full(int stream_id, string
sequence, string flag [, int options])
```
   Set flags on messages

```
array imap_sort(int stream_id, int criteria, int
reverse [, int options])
```
   Sort an array of message headers

```
object imap_status(int stream_id, string mailbox,
int options)
```
   Get status info from a mailbox

```
int imap_subscribe(int stream_id, string mailbox)
```
   Subscribe to a mailbox

```
int imap_uid(int stream_id, int msg_no)
```
   Get the unique message ID associated with a standard
   sequential message number

```
int imap_undelete(int stream_id, int msg_no)
```
   Remove the delete flag from a message

```
int imap_unsubscribe(int stream_id, string
mailbox)
```
   Unsubscribe from a mailbox

LDAP Functions

The following functions are used to communicate with a
Lightweight Directory Access Protocol (LDAP) server. See

---

http://www.openldap.org for a PHP-compatible free LDAP implementation.

```
int ldap_add(int link, string dn, array entry)
```
Add entries to an LDAP directory

```
int ldap_bind(int link [, string dn, string password])
```
Bind to an LDAP directory

```
int ldap_close(int link)
```
Alias for ldap_unbind()

```
int ldap_connect([string host [, int port]])
```
Connect to an LDAP server

```
int ldap_count_entries(int link, int result)
```
Count the number of entries in a search result

```
int ldap_delete(int link, string dn)
```
Delete an entry from a directory

```
string ldap_dn2ufn(string dn)
```
Convert a distinguished name to a user friendly naming format

```
string ldap_err2str(int errno)
```
Convert error number to error string

```
int ldap_errno(int link)
```
Get the current LDAP error number

```
string ldap_error(int link)
```
Get the current LDAP error string

```
array ldap_explode_dn(string dn, int with_attrib)
```
Split a distinguished name into its component parts

```
string ldap_first_attribute(int link, int result, int ber)
```
Return the first attribute

```
int ldap_first_entry(int link, int result)
```
Return the first result ID

```
int ldap_free_result(int result)
```
Free result memory

```
array ldap_get_attributes(int link, int result)
```
Get attributes from a search result entry

```
string ldap_get_dn(int link, int result)
```
Get the distinguished name of a result entry

```
array ldap_get_entries(int link, int result)
```
Get all result entries

```
array ldap_get_values(int link, int result,
string attribute)
```
Get all values from a result entry

```
array ldap_get_values_len(int link, int result,
string attribute)
```
Get all values from a result entry

```
int ldap_list(int link, string base_dn, string
filter [, string attributes])
```
Single-level search

```
int ldap_mod_add(int link, string dn, array
entry)
```
Add attribute values to current entry

```
int ldap_mod_del(int link, string dn, array
entry)
```
Delete attribute values

```
int ldap_mod_replace(int link, string dn, array
entry)
```
Replace attribute values with new ones

```
int ldap_modify(int link, string dn, array entry)
```
Modify an LDAP entry

```
string ldap_next_attribute(int link, int result,
int ber)
```
Get the next attribute in result

```
int ldap_next_entry(int link, int entry)
```
Get the next result entry

```
int ldap_read(int link, string base_dn, string
filter [, string attributes])
```
Read an entry

```
int ldap_search(int link, string base_dn, string
filter [, string attributes])
```
Search LDAP tree under the base_dn

```
int ldap_unbind(int link)
```
Unbind from an LDAP directory

Math Functions

There are two types of math functions in PHP. The first
type is the standard functions that operate on regular numbers. The scope and precision of these functions is limited
by the operating system:

```
int abs(int number)
```
Return the absolute value of the number

```
double acos(double number)
```
Return the arc cosine of the number in radians

```
double asin(double number)
```
Return the arc sine of the number in radians

```
double atan(double number)
```
Return the arc tangent of the number in radians

```
double atan2(double y, double x)
```
Return the arc tangent of y/x, with the resulting quad-
rant determined by the signs of y and x

```
string base_convert(string number, int from-
base, int tobase)
```
Convert a number in a string from any base to any oth-
er base (where both bases are less than or equal to 36)

```
int bindec(string binary_number)
```
Return the decimal equivalent of the binary number

```
int ceil(double number)
```
Return the next higher integer value of the number

```
double cos(double number)
```
Return the cosine of the number in radians

```
string decbin(int decimal_number)
```
Return a string containing a binary representation of the number

```
string dechex(int decimal_number)
```
Return a string containing a hexadecimal representation of the given number

```
string decoct(int octal_number)
```
Return a string containing an octal representation of the given number

```
double deg2rad(double degrees)
```
Convert the number in degrees to the radian equivalent

```
double exp(double number)
```
Return *e* raised to the power of the number

```
int floor(double number)
```
Return the next lower integer value from the number

```
int hexdec(string hexadecimal_number)
```
Return the decimal equivalent of the hexadecimal number

```
double log(double number)
```
Return the natural logarithm of the number

```
double log10(double number)
```
Return the base-10 logarithm of the number

```
string number_format(double number [, int num_
decimal_places [, string dec_seperator, string
thousands_seperator)]])
```
Format a number with grouped thousands

```
int octdec(string octal_number)
```
Return the decimal equivalent of an octal string

```
double pi(void)
```
Return an approximation of π

```
double pow(double base, double exponent)
```
Return base raised to the power of exponent

```
double rad2deg(double radians)
```
Convert the radian number to the equivalent number in degrees

```
double round(double number)
```
Return the rounded value of the number

```
double sin(double number)
```
Return the sine of the number in radians

```
double sqrt(double number)
```
Return the square root of the number

```
double tan(double number)
```
Return the tangent of the number in radians

BC Arbitrary Precision Math Functions

The second type of math functions is the BC set of functions. These are arbitrary precision functions where the numbers themselves are stored as strings. The BC functions act on these strings. The benefit of using these functions is that there is no limit to the size or precision of the numbers you are working with:

```
string bcadd(string left_operand, string right_
operand [, int scale])
```
Return the sum of two arbitrary precision numbers

```
string bccomp(string left_operand, string right_
operand [, int scale])
```
Compare two arbitrary precision numbers

```
string bcdiv(string left_operand, string right_
operand [, int scale])
```
Return the result of dividing two arbitrary precision numbers

```
string bcmod(string left_operand, string modulus)
```
Return the modulus of an arbitrary precision number

```
string bcmul(string left_operand, string right_
operand [, int scale])
```
Return the product of two arbitrary precision numbers

```
string bcpow(string x, string y [, int scale])
```
Return the value of one arbitrary precision number raised to the power of another

```
string bcscale(int scale)
```
Set the default scale parameter for all BC math functions

```
string bcsqrt(string operand [, int scale])
```
Return the square root of an arbitrary precision number

```
string bcsub(string left_operand, string right_
operand [, int scale])
```
Return the result of subtracting one arbitrary precision number from another

MCAL Functions

The MCAL library, available at *http://mcal.chek.com*, is used to connect to calendars. MCAL supports different protocols, including ICAP. Note that these functions supercede the icap_ functions in PHP:

```
int mcal_close(int stream_id [, int options])
```
Close an MCAL stream

```
string mcal_create_calendar(int stream_id, string
calendar)
```
Create a new calendar

```
bool mcal_date_valid(int year, int month, int
day)
```
   Return true if the date is a valid date

```
int mcal_day_of_week(int ayear, int amonth, int
aday, int byear, int bmonth,int bday)
```
   Compare two dates

```
int mcal_day_of_week(int year, int month, int
day)
```
   Return the day of the week of the given date

```
int mcal_day_of_year(int year, int month, int
day)
```
   Return the day of the year of the given date

```
int mcal_days_in_month(int month, bool leap_
year)
```
   Return the number of days in the given month (needs to
   know if the year is a leap year or not)

```
string mcal_delete_calendar(int stream_id, string
calendar)
```
   Delete calendar

```
string mcal_delete_event(int stream_id, int uid)
```
   Delete event

```
int mcal_event_init(int stream_id)
```
   Initialize a stream's global event

```
int mcal_event_set_alarm(int stream_id, int
alarm)
```
   Add an alarm to the stream's global event

```
string mcal_event_set_category(int stream_id,
string category)
```
   Attach a category to an event

```
int mcal_event_set_class(int stream_id, int
class)
```
   Add a class to the stream's global event

```
string mcal_event_set_description(int stream_id,
string description)
```
Attach a description to an event

```
string mcal_event_set_end(int stream_id, int
year, int month, int day, [[[int hour], int
min], int sec])
```
Attach an end date/time to an event

```
int mcal_event_set_now(int stream_id)
```
Set a stream's global event end date to the current date/
time

```
int mcal_event_set_now(int stream_id)
```
Set a stream's global event start date to the current date/
time

```
string mcal_event_set_recur_daily(int stream_id,
int year, int month, int day, int interval)
```
Create a daily recurrence

```
string mcal_event_set_recur_monthly_mday (int
stream_id, int year, int month, int day, int
interval)
```
Create a monthly-by-day recurrence

```
string mcal_event_set_recur_monthly_wday (int
stream_id, int year, int month, int day, int
interval)
```
Create a monthly-by-week recurrence

```
string mcal_event_set_recur_weekly(int stream_
id, int year, int month, int day, int interval,
int weekdays)
```
Create a weekly recurrence

```
string mcal_event_set_recur_yearly(int stream_
id, int year, int month, int day, int interval)
```
Create a yearly recurrence

```
string mcal_event_set_start(int stream_id, int
year,int month, int day, [[[int hour], int min],
int sec])
```
   Attach a start date/time to an event

```
string mcal_event_set_title(int stream_id, string
title)
```
   Attach a title to an event

```
int mcal_expunge(int stream_id)
```
   Delete all messages marked for deletion

```
object mcal_fetch_current_stream_event (int
stream_id)
```
   Fetch the current event stored in the stream's event
   structure

```
int mcal_fetch_event(int stream_id, int eventid,
[int options])
```
   Fetch an event

```
bool mcal_is_leap_year(int year)
```
   Return true if year is a leap year, false if not

```
int mcal_list_alarms(int stream_id, int year, int
month, int day, int hour, int min, int sec)
```
   List alarms for a given time

```
array mcal_list_events(int stream_id, int start-
year, int startmonth, int startday, int endyear,
int endmonth, int endday)
```
   Return list of events for a day or range of days

```
object mcal_next_recurrence(int stream_id, int
weekstart, array next)
```
   Return an object filled with the next date the event
   occurs, on or after the supplied date

```
int mcal_open(string calendar, string user,
string password [, int options])
```
   Open an MCAL stream to a calendar

```
string mcal_rename(int stream_id, string src_
calendar, string dest_calendar)
```
Rename a calendar

```
int mcal_reopen(int stream_id, string calendar [,
int options])
```
Reopen an MCAL stream to a new calendar

```
string mcal_snooze(int stream_id, int uid)
```
Snooze an alarm

```
string mcal_store_event(int stream_id, object
event)
```
Store an event

```
bool mcal_time_valid(int hour,int min,int sec)
```
Return true if the time is a valid time

Mcrypt Functions

The *mcrypt* library available at *ftp://argeas.cs-net.gr/pub/ unix/mcrypt* supports a wide variety of block algorithms such as DES, TripleDES, Blowfish (default), 3-WAY, SAFER-SK64, SAFER-SK128, TWOFISH, TEA, RC2 and GOST in CBC, OFB, CFB, and ECB cipher modes. Additionally, it supports RC6 and IDEA, which are considered "non-free":

```
int mcrypt_cbc(int cipher, string key, string
data, int mode [,string iv])
```
CBC crypt/decrypt data using key with cipher and optional iv

```
int mcrypt_cfb(int cipher, string key, string
data, int mode, string iv)
```
CFB crypt/decrypt data using key with cipher starting with iv

```
string mcrypt_create_iv(int size, int source)
```
Create an initializing vector (IV)

```
int mcrypt_ecb(int cipher, string key, string
data, int mode)
```
ECB crypt/decrypt data using key with cipher

```
int mcrypt_get_block_size(int cipher)
```
Get the block size of a cipher

```
string mcrypt_get_cipher_name(int cipher)
```
Get the name of a cipher

```
int mcrypt_get_key_size(int cipher)
```
Get the key size of a cipher

```
int mcrypt_ofb(int cipher, string key, string
data, int mode, string iv)
```
OFB crypt/decrypt data using `key` with `cipher` starting
with `iv`

Mhash Functions

The *mhash* library available at *http://sasweb.de/mhash/* supports a wide variety of hash algorithms, including MD5,
SHA1, GOST, and many others:

```
string mhash(int hash, string data)
```
Hash data with `hash`

```
int mhash_count(void)
```
Get the number of available hashes

```
int mhash_get_block_size(int hash)
```
Get the block size of `hash`

```
string mhash_get_hash_name(int hash)
```
Get the name of `hash`

Networking Functions

DNS and Socket Functions

```
int checkdnsrr(string host [, string type])
```
Check DNS records corresponding to a given Internet
hostname or IP address

```
int fsockopen(string hostname, int port [, int
errno [, string errstr [, int timeout]]])
```
Open Internet or Unix domain socket connection

```
string gethostbyaddr(string ip_address)
```
Get the Internet hostname corresponding to a given IP address

```
string gethostbyname(string hostname)
```
Get the IP address corresponding to a given Internet hostname

```
array gethostbynamel(string hostname)
```
Return a list of IP addresses that a given hostname resolves to

```
int getmxrr(string hostname, array mxhosts [,
array weight])
```
Get MX records corresponding to a given Internet hostname

```
int pfsockopen(string hostname, int port [, int
errno [, string errstr [, int timeout]]])
```
Open persistent Internet or Unix domain socket connection

```
int set_socket_blocking(int socket descriptor,
int mode)
```
Set blocking/non-blocking mode on a socket

FTP Functions

```
int ftp_cdup(int stream)
```
Change to the parent directory

```
int ftp_chdir(int stream, string directory)
```
Change directories

```
int ftp_connect(string host [, int port])
```
Open an FTP stream

```
int ftp_delete(int stream, string path)
```
Delete a file

```
int ftp_fget(int stream, int fp, string remote_
file, int mode)
```
  Retrieve a file from the FTP server and write it to an
  open file

```
int ftp_fput(int stream, string local_file,
string remote_file, int mode)
```
  Store a file from an open file to the FTP server

```
int ftp_get(int stream, string local_file, string
remote_file, int mode)
```
  Retrieve a file from the FTP server and write it to a local
  file

```
int ftp_login(int stream, string username, string
password)
```
  Log into the FTP server

```
int ftp_mdtm(int stream, string path)
```
  Return the last modification time of the file, or −1 on
  error

```
string ftp_mkdir(int stream, string directory)
```
  Create a directory

```
array ftp_nlist(int stream, string directory)
```
  Return an array of filenames in the given directory

```
int ftp_pasv(int stream, int pasv)
```
  Turn passive mode on or off

```
int ftp_put(int stream, string remote_file,
string local_file, int mode)
```
  Store a file on the FTP server

```
string ftp_pwd(int stream)
```
  Return the present working directory

```
int ftp_quit(int stream)
```
  Close the FTP stream

```
array ftp_rawlist(int stream, string directory)
```
  Return a detailed listing of a directory as an array of output lines

---

```
int ftp_rename(int stream, string src, string
dest)
```
   Rename the given file to a new path

```
int ftp_rmdir(int stream, string directory)
```
   Remove a directory

```
int ftp_size(int stream, string path)
```
   Return the size of the file, or -1 on error

```
string ftp_systype(int stream)
```
   Return the system type identifier

NIS Functions

```
array yp_first(string domain, string map)
```
   Return the first key as $var["key"] and the first line as
   $var["value"]

```
string yp_get_default_domain(void)
```
   Return the domain or false

```
string yp_master(string domain, string map)
```
   Return the machine name of the master

```
string yp_match(string domain, string map, string
key)
```
   Return the matched line or false

```
array yp_next(string domain, string map, string
key)
```
   Return an array with $var[$key] and the line as the
   value

```
int yp_order(string domain, string map)
```
   Return the order number or false

SNMP Functions

```
int snmp_get_quick_print(void)
```
   Return the current status of quick_print

```
void snmp_set_quick_print(int quick_print)
```
   Set quick_print

```
string snmpget(string host, string community,
string object_id [, int timeout [, int
retries]])
```
   Fetch an SNMP object

```
array snmprealwalk(string host, string commu-
nity, string object_id[, int timeout[, int
retries]])
```
   An alias for snmpwalkoid()

```
int snmpset(string host, string community, string
object_id, string type, mixed value [, int
timeout [, int retries]])
```
   Set the value of a SNMP object

```
string snmpwalk(string host, string community,
string object_id [, int timeout [, int
retries]])
```
   Return all objects under the specified object ID

```
array snmpwalkoid(string host, string commu-
nity, string object_id [, int timeout [, int
retries]])
```
   Return an associative array of object ID/value pairs of all
   objects under the specified one

PDF Functions

PHP provides functions that can be used to create Adobe
Portable Document Format (PDF) files on the fly. See *http://
www.pdflib.com/* for the required *pdflib* library and associated documentation.

ClibPDF is an alternate PDF generation library available at
http://www.fastio.com. PHP also supports ClibPDF, with
functions that begin with cpdf_ and are very similar to the
regular pdf_ functions.

```
void pdf_add_annotation(int pdfdoc, double xll,
double yll, double xur, double xur, string
title, string text)
```
Set annotation

```
void pdf_add_outline(int pdfdoc, string text);
```
Add bookmark for current page

```
void pdf_add_pdflink(int pdfdoc, double llx,
double lly, double urx, double ury, string file-
name, int page, string dest)
```
Add link to PDF document

```
void pdf_add_weblink(int pdfdoc, double llx,
double lly, double urx, double ury, string url)
```
Add link to web resource

```
void pdf_arc(int pdfdoc, double x, double y,
double radius, double start, double end)
```
Draw an arc

```
void pdf_begin_page(int pdfdoc, double height,
double width)
```
Start page

```
void pdf_circle(int pdfdoc, double x, double y,
double radius)
```
Draw a circle

```
void pdf_clip(int pdfdoc)
```
Clip to current path

```
void pdf_close(int pdfdoc)
```
Close the PDF document

```
void pdf_close_image(int pdfimage)
```
Close the PDF image

```
void pdf_closepath(int pdfdoc)
```
Close path

```
void pdf_closepath_fill_stroke(int pdfdoc)
```
Close, fill, and stroke current path

```
void pdf_closepath_stroke(int pdfdoc)
```
Close path and draw line along path

```
void pdf_continue_text(int pdfdoc, string text)
```
Output text in next line

```
void pdf_curveto(int pdfdoc, double x1, double
y1, double x2, double y2, double x3, double y3)
```
Draw a curve

```
void pdf_end_page(int pdfdoc)
```
End page

```
void pdf_endpath(int pdfdoc)
```
End current path

```
void pdf_execute_image(int pdf, int pdfimage, int
x, int y, int scale)
```
Place stored image in the PDF document

```
void pdf_fill(int pdfdoc)
```
Fill current path

```
void pdf_fill_stroke(int pdfdoc)
```
Fill and stroke current path

```
void pdf_get_image_height(int pdf, int pdfimage)
```
Return the height of an image

```
void pdf_get_image_width(int pdf, int pdfimage)
```
Return the width of an image

```
int pdf_get_info(void)
```
Return a default info structure for a PDF document

```
void pdf_lineto(int pdfdoc, double x, double y)
```
Draw a line

```
void pdf_moveto(int pdfdoc, double x, double y)
```
Set current point

```
int pdf_open(int filedesc, int info)
```
Open a new PDF document

```
int pdf_open_gif(int pdf, string giffile)
```
Open a GIF file and return an image for placement in a PDF document

```
int pdf_open_jpeg(int pdf, string jpegfile)
```
Open a JPEG file and return an image for placement in a PDF document

```
int pdf_open_memory_image(int pdf, int image)
```
Take a GD image and return an image for placement in a PDF document

```
void pdf_place_image(int pdf, int pdfimage, int
x, int y, int scale)
```
Place image in the PDF document

```
void pdf_put_image(int pdf, int pdfimage)
```
Store image in the PDF document for later use

```
void pdf_rect(int pdfdoc, double x, double y,
double width, double height)
```
Draw a rectangle

```
void pdf_restore(int pdfdoc)
```
Restore formerly saved environment

```
void pdf_rotate(int pdfdoc, double angle)
```
Set rotation

```
void pdf_save(int pdfdoc)
```
Save current environment

```
void pdf_scale(int pdfdoc, double x-scale, double
y-scale)
```
Set scaling

```
void pdf_set_border_color(int pdfdoc, double red,
double green, double blue)
```
Set color of box surrounding web links

```
void pdf_set_border_style(int pdfdoc, string
style, double width)
```
Set style of box surrounding web links

```
void pdf_set_char_spacing(int pdfdoc, double
space)
```
Set character spacing

```
void pdf_set_duration(int pdfdoc, double
duration)
```
Set duration between pages

```
void pdf_set_font(int pdfdoc, string font, double
size, string encoding [, int embed])
```
Select the current font face and size

```
void pdf_set_horiz_scaling(int pdfdoc, double
scale)
```
Set horizontal scaling of text

```
pdf_set_info_author(int info, string author)
```
Fill the author field of the info structure

```
pdf_set_info_creator(int info, string creator)
```
Fill the creator field of the info structure

```
pdf_set_info_keywords(int info, string keywords)
```
Fill the keywords field of the info structure

```
pdf_set_info_subject(int info, string subject)
```
Fill the subject field of the info structure

```
pdf_set_info_title(int info, string title)
```
Fill the title field of the info structure

```
void pdf_set_leading(int pdfdoc, double distance)
```
Set distance between text lines

```
void pdf_set_text_matrix(int pdfdoc, arry matrix)
```
Set the text matrix

```
void pdf_set_text_pos(int pdfdoc, double x,
double y)
```
Set text position

```
void pdf_set_text_rendering(int pdfdoc, int mode)
```
Determine how text is rendered

```
void pdf_set_text_rise(int pdfdoc, double value)
```
Set the text rise

```
void pdf_set_transition(int pdfdoc, int
transition)
```
Set transition between pages

```
void pdf_set_word_spacing(int pdfdoc, double
space)
```
Set spacing between words

```
void pdf_setdash(int pdfdoc, double white, double
black)
```
Set dash pattern

```
void pdf_setflat(int pdfdoc, double value)
```
Set flatness

```
void pdf_setgray(int pdfdoc, double value)
```
Set drawing and filling color to gray value

```
void pdf_setgray_fill(int pdfdoc, double value)
```
Set filling color to gray value

```
void pdf_setgray_stroke(int pdfdoc, double value)
```
Set drawing color to gray value

```
void pdf_setlinecap(int pdfdoc, int value)
```
Set linecap parameter

```
void pdf_setlinejoin(int pdfdoc, int value)
```
Set linejoin parameter

```
void pdf_setlinewidth(int pdfdoc, double width)
```
Set line width

```
void pdf_setmiterlimit(int pdfdoc, double value)
```
Set miter limit

```
void pdf_setrgbcolor(int pdfdoc, double red,
double green, double blue)
```
Set drawing and filling color to RGB color value

```
void pdf_setrgbcolor_fill(int pdfdoc, double red,
double green, double blue)
```
Set filling color to RGB color value

```
void pdf_setrgbcolor_stroke(int pdfdoc, double
red, double green, double blue)
```
   Set drawing color to RGB color value

```
void pdf_show(int pdfdoc, string text)
```
   Output text at current position

```
void pdf_show_xy(int pdfdoc, string text, double
x, double y)
```
   Output text at position

```
double pdf_stringwidth(int pdfdoc, string text)
```
   Return width of text in current font

```
void pdf_stroke(int pdfdoc)
```
   Draw line along path

```
void pdf_translate(int pdfdoc, double x, double
y)
```
   Set origin of coordinate system

FDF

Forms Data Format (FDF) is a format for handling forms
within PDF documents. Refer to *http://partners.adobe.com/
asn/developer/acrosdk/main.html* for more information
about FDF:

```
void fdf_add_template(int fdfdoc, int newpage,
string filename, string template, int rename)
```
   Add a template to the FDF document

```
void fdf_close(int fdfdoc)
```
   Close the FDF document

```
void fdf_create(void)
```
   Create a new FDF document

```
void fdf_get_file(int fdfdoc)
```
   Get the value in the /F key

```
void fdf_get_status(int fdfdoc)
```
   Get the value in the /Status key

```
void fdf_get_value(int fdfdoc, string fieldname)
```
   Get the value of a field as string

```
void fdf_next_field_name(int fdfdoc [, string
fieldname])
```
   Get the name of the next field name or the first field name

```
int fdf_open(string filename)
```
   Open a new FDF document

```
void fdf_save(int fdfdoc, string filename)
```
   Write out an FDF file

```
void fdf_set_ap(int fdfdoc, string fieldname, int
face, string filename, int pagenr)
```
   Set the value of a field

```
void fdf_set_file(int fdfdoc, string filename)
```
   Set the value in the /F key

```
void fdf_set_status(int fdfdoc, string status)
```
   Set the value in the /Status key

```
void fdf_set_value(int fdfdoc, string field-
name, string value, int isName)
```
   Set the value of a field

POSIX Functions

These functions conform to the IEEE 1003.1 (POSIX.1) standard:

```
string posix_ctermid(void)
```
   Generate terminal path name (POSIX.1, 4.7.1)

```
string posix_getcwd()
```
   Get working directory pathname (POSIX.1, 5.2.2)

```
long posix_getegid(void)
```
   Get the current effective group ID (POSIX.1, 4.2.1)

```
long posix_geteuid(void)
```
   Get the current effective user ID (POSIX.1, 4.2.1)

```
```

```
long posix_getgid(void)
```
Get the current group ID (POSIX.1, 4.2.1)

```
array posix_getgrgid(long gid)
```
Group database access (POSIX.1, 9.2.1)

```
array posix_getgrnam(string groupname)
```
Group database access (POSIX.1, 9.2.1)

```
long posix_getgroups(void)
```
Get supplementary group IDs (POSIX.1, 4.2.3)

```
string posix_getlogin(void)
```
Get user name (POSIX.1, 4.2.4)

```
long posix_getpgid(void)
```
Get the process group ID of the specified process (non-POSIX)

```
long posix_getpgrp(void)
```
Get current process group ID (POSIX.1, 4.3.1)

```
long posix_getpid(void)
```
Get the current process ID (POSIX.1, 4.1.1)

```
long posix_getppid(void)
```
Get the parent process ID (POSIX.1, 4.1.1)

```
array posix_getpwnam(string groupname)
```
User database access (POSIX.1, 9.2.2)

```
array posix_getpwuid(long uid)
```
User database access (POSIX.1, 9.2.2)

```
long posix_getrlimit(void)
```
Get system resource consumption limits (non-POSIX)

```
long posix_getsid(void)
```
Get process group ID of session leader (non-POSIX)

```
long posix_getuid(void)
```
Get the current user ID (POSIX.1, 4.2.1)

```
bool posix_isatty(int fd)
```
Determine if file descriptor is a tty (POSIX.1, 4.7.1)

```
int posix_kill(int pid, int sig)
```
   Send a signal to a process (POSIX.1, 3.3.2)

```
string posix_mkfifo()
```
   Make a FIFO special file (POSIX.1, 5.4.2)

```
long posix_setgid(long uid)
```
   Set group ID (POSIX.1, 4.2.2)

```
long posix_setpgid(long pid, long pgid)
```
   Set process group ID for job control (POSIX.1, 4.3.3)

```
long posix_setsid(void)
```
   Create session and set process group ID (POSIX.1, 4.3.2)

```
long posix_setuid(long uid)
```
   Set user ID (POSIX.1, 4.2.2)

```
array posix_times(void)
```
   Get process times (POSIX.1, 4.5.2)

```
string posix_ttyname(int fd)
```
   Determine terminal device name (POSIX.1, 4.7.2)

```
array posix_uname(void)
```
   Get system name (POSIX.1, 4.4.1)

String Functions

These are the basic string manipulation functions supported by PHP. They are all 8-bit clean, which means that the data they act on does not necessarily have to be straight text. In other words, a string may include any character in the ASCII table including 0. Here are the string functions:

```
string addslashes(string str)
```
   Escape single quotes, double quotes, and backslash characters in a string with backslashes

```
string base64_decode(string str)
```
   Decode a string with MIME base-64

```
string base64_encode(string str)
```
   Encode a string with MIME base-64

```
string chop(string str)
```
Remove trailing whitespace

```
string chr(int ascii)
```
Convert an ASCII code to a character

```
string chunk_split(string str [, int chunklen [,
string ending]])
```
Return split line

```
string convert_cyr_string(string str, string
from, string to)
```
Convert from one Cyrillic character set to another

```
string crypt(string str [, string salt])
```
DES-encrypt a string

```
string decrypt(string data, int type, string key)
```
Decrypt string with key using algorithm type (converse
of encrypt())

```
string encrypt(string data, int type, string key)
```
Encrypts string with key using algorithm type (converse of decrypt())

```
int ereg(string pattern, string string [, array
registers])
```
POSIX-style regular expression match

```
string ereg_replace(string pattern, string string
[, array registers])
```
Replace pattern in a string using a POSIX-style regular
expression

```
int eregi(string pattern, string string [, array
registers])
```
Case-insensitive POSIX-style regular expression match

```
string eregi_replace(string pattern, string
string [, array registers])
```
Case insensitive POSIX-style replace regular expression

```
array explode(string separator, string str)
```
Split a string on the specified string separator

```
string gamma_correct_tag(string color, double
inputgamma, double outputgamma)
```
Apply a gamma correction to a HTML color value
(#rrggbb)

```
string hebrev(string str, int max_chars_per_
line)
```
Convert logical Hebrew text to visual text

```
string hebrevc(string str, int max_chars_per_
line)
```
Convert logical Hebrew text to visual text with newline
conversion

```
string htmlentities(string str)
```
Convert all applicable characters to HTML entities

```
string htmlspecialchars(string str)
```
Convert special characters to HTML entities

```
string implode(array src, string glue)
```
Join array elements into a string

```
string join(string glue, array src)
```
Join array elements into a string

```
string ltrim(string str)
```
Strip whitespace from the beginning of a string

```
string md5(string str)
```
Calculate the md5 hash of a string

```
string nl2br(string str)
```
Converts newlines to HTML line breaks

```
int ord(string character)
```
Return the ASCII value of character

```
void parse_str(string str)
```
Parse the string into variables

```
int preg_match(string pattern, string subject [,
array subpatterns ])
```
Perform a Perl-style regular expression match

```
int preg_match_all(string pattern, string
subject, array subpatterns [, int order ])
```
Perform a Perl-style global regular expression match

```
string preg_quote(string str)
```
Quote Perl-style regular expression characters

```
string preg_replace(string|array regex,
string|array replace, string|array subject)
```
Perform Perl-style regular expression replacement

```
array preg_split(string pattern, string subject
[, int limit ])
```
Split string into an array using a Perl-style regular expression as a delimiter

```
void print(string str)
```
Output a string

```
int printf(string format, mixed args, ...)
```
Output a formatted string

```
string quoted_printable_decode(string str)
```
Convert a quoted-printable string to an 8-bit string

```
string quotemeta(string str)
```
Quote metacharacters

```
string rawurldecode(string str)
```
Decode URL-encoded strings

```
string rawurlencode(string str)
```
URL-encode according to RFC-1738

```
string rtrim(string str)
```
Remove trailing whitespace (alias for chop( ) function)

```
string setlocale(string category, string locale)
```
Set locale information

```
int similar_text(string str1, string str2 [,
double percent])
```
Calculate the similarity between two strings

```
string soundex(string str)
```
Calculate the soundex key of a string

```
array split(string pattern, string string [, int
limit])
```
Split string into array by a POSIX-style regular expression

```
string sprintf(string format, mixed args, ...)
```
Return a formatted string

```
string sql_regcase(string string)
```
Make regular expression for case-insensitive match

```
string str_replace(string needle, string str,
string haystack)
```
Replace all occurrences of needle in haystack with str

```
int strcasecmp(string str1, string str2)
```
Binary safe, case-insensitive string comparison

```
string strchr(string haystack, string needle)
```
Find the last occurrence of a character in a string

```
int strcmp(string str1, string str2)
```
Binary safe string comparison

```
int strcspn(string str1, string str2)
```
Find length of initial segment not matching mask

```
string strip_tags(string str [, string allowable_
tags])
```
Strip HTML and PHP tags from a string

```
string stripslashes(string str)
```
Unquote string quoted with addslashes( )

```
string stristr(string haystack, string needle)
```
Find first occurrence of a string within another (case-insensitive)

```
int strlen(string str)
```
Get string length

```
int strpos(string haystack, string needle)
```
Find position of first occurrence of a string

```
string strrchr(string haystack, string needle)
```
Find the last occurrence of a character in a string

```
string strrev(string str)
```
Reverse a string

```
int strrpos(string haystack, string needle)
```
Find position of last occurrence of a character in a string

```
int strspn(string str1, string str2)
```
Find length of initial segment matching mask

```
string strstr(string haystack, string needle)
```
Find first occurrence of a string

```
string strtok(string str, string token)
```
Tokenize string

```
string strtolower(string str)
```
Make a string lowercase

```
string strtoupper(string str)
```
Make a string uppercase

```
string strtr(string str, string from, string to)
```
Translate certain characters

```
string substr(string str, int start, int length)
```
Return part of a string

```
string trim(string str)
```
Strip whitespace from the beginning and end of a string

```
string ucfirst(string str)
```
Make a string's first character uppercase

```
string ucwords(string str)
```
Uppercase the first character of every word in a string

```
string uniqid(string prefix [, bool more_
entropy])
```
Generate a unique ID

```
string urldecode(string str)
```
Decode URL-encoded string

```
string urlencode(string str)
```
URL-encode a string

Variable Manipulation Functions

The following functions operate on PHP variables. There are functions for getting and setting the type of a variable, as well as various ways to encode and decode variables for storage.

```
bool define(string var_name, mixed value[, int
case_sensitive])
```
   Define a constant value

```
int defined(string constant_name)
```
   Test if a constant is defined

```
double doubleval(mixed var)
```
   Get the double-precision value of a variable

```
string getenv(string varname)
```
   Get the value of an environment variable

```
string gettype(mixed var)
```
   Return the type of the variable

```
int intval(mixed var [, int base])
```
   Get the integer value of a variable using the optional base for the conversion

```
bool is_array(mixed var)
```
   Return true if variable is an array

```
bool is_double(mixed var)
```
   Return true if variable is a double

```
bool is_float(mixed var)
```
   An alias for is_double( )

```
bool is_int(mixed var)
```
   An alias for is_long( )

```
bool is_integer(mixed var)
```
   An alias for is_long( )

```
bool is_long(mixed var)
```
Return true if variable is a long (integer)

```
bool is_object(mixed var)
```
Return true if variable is an object

```
bool is_real(mixed var)
```
An alias for is_double( )

```
bool is_string(mixed var)
```
Return true if variable is a string

```
string pack(string format, mixed arg1, mixed
arg2, ...)
```
Take one or more arguments and pack them into a binary string according to the format argument

```
bool is_real(mixed var)
```
An alias for is_double( )

```
bool is_string(mixed var)
```
Return true if variable is a string

```
void putenv(string setting)
```
Set the value of an environment variable

```
string serialize(mixed variable)
```
Return a string representation of variable (which can later be unserialized)

```
int settype(string var, string type)
```
Set the type of the variable

```
string strval(mixed var)
```
Get the string value of a variable

```
array unpack(string format, string input)
```
Unpack binary string into named array elements according to format argument

```
mixed unserialize(string variable_
representation)
```
Take a string representation of variable and recreate it

```
void var_dump(mixed var)
```
Dump a string representation of variable to output

XML Functions

As of Version 3.0.6, PHP has XML support built on top of James Clark's *expat* library.

XML Event Handlers

PHP's XML support is event driven. This means that it lets you set up functions that can handle different types of data from the parser. Here are the different types of handlers:

Element handlers
Called when the parser encounters start and end elements (tags).

Character data handler
Called when non-markup character data is found.

Processing instruction (PI) handler
Called for processing instruction information. PHP code, among other things, can be embedded into such markup.

Notation declaration handler
Called for notation definitions (notations are a way of declaring data formats).

External entity reference handler and unparsed entity declaration handler
Called for entity references and declarations.

Default handler
Called for data that is not covered by any other handler.

Character Encoding

The XML extension supports three character sets: US-ASCII, ISO-8859-1, and UTF-8 encoded Unicode. Input (source)

---

and output (target) encoding can be controlled separately. UTF-16 is not supported.

XML Functions

`string utf8_decode(string data)`
  Convert a UTF-8 encoded string to ISO-8859-1

`string utf8_encode(string data)`
  Encode an ISO-8859-1 string to UTF-8

`string xml_error_string(int code)`
  Get XML parser error string

`int xml_get_current_byte_index(int parser)`
  Get the current byte index for the XML parser

`int xml_get_current_column_number(int parser)`
  Get the current column number for the XML parser

`int xml_get_current_line_number(int parser)`
  Get the current line number for the XML parser

`int xml_get_error_code(int parser)`
  Get the XML parser error code

`int xml_parse(int parser, string data[, int is_final])`
  Start parsing an XML document

`int xml_parse_into_struct(int pind, string data,array &struct,array &index)`
  Parse an XML document

`int xml_parser_create([string encoding])`
  Create an XML parser and return a handle for use by other XML functions

`string xml_parser_free(int parser)`
  Free the XML parser

`mixed xml_parser_get_option(int parser, int option)`
  Get options from the XML parser

```
int xml_parser_set_option(int parser, int option,
mixed value)
```
Set options in the XML parser

```
int xml_set_character_data_handler(int parser,
string handler)
```
Set the character data handler function for the XML
parser

```
int xml_set_default_handler(int parser, string
handler)
```
Set the default handler function for the XML parser

```
int xml_set_element_handler(int parser, string
shandler, string handler)
```
Set the element handler functions for the XML parser

```
int xml_set_external_entity_ref_handler (int
parser, string handler)
```
Set the notation declaration handler function for the
XML parser

```
int xml_set_notation_decl_handler(int parser,
string handler)
```
Set the notation declaration handler function for the
XML parser

```
int xml_set_processing_instruction_handler (int
parser, string handler)
```
Set the processing instruction (PI) handler function for
the XML parser

```
int xml_set_unparsed_entity_decl_handler (int
parser, string handler)
```
Set the unparsed entity declaration handler function for
the XML parser

WDDX

WDDX is an XML-based technology that supports the
exchange of complex data between web programming languages. With WDDX, you can serialize data to some

---

storage mechanism and then read it back into PHP or
another WDDX-compliant language later.

```
int wddx_add_vars(int packet_id, ...)
```
Serialize given variables and add them to packet given
by `packet_id`

```
mixed wddx_deserialize(string packet)
```
Deserialize given packet and return a PHP value

```
string wddx_packet_end(int packet_id)
```
End specified WDDX packet and return the string containing the packet

```
int wddx_packet_start([ string comment ])
```
Start a WDDX packet with optional comment and return
the packet ID

```
string wddx_serialize_value(mixed var [, string
comment ])
```
Create a new packet and serialize the given value

```
string wddx_serialize_vars(...)
```
Create a new packet and serialize given variables into a
structure

Miscellaneous Functions

Program Execution Functions

```
escapeshellcmd(string command)
```
Escape shell metacharacters

```
int exec(string command [, array output [, int
return_value]])
```
Execute an external program

```
int passthru(string command [, int return_
value])
```
Execute an external program and display raw output

```
int system(string command [, int return_value])
```
Execute an external program and display output

Random Number Functions

```
int getrandmax(void)
```
Return the maximum value a random number can have

```
int mt_getrandmax(void)
```
Return the maximum value a random number from Mersenne Twister can have

```
int mt_rand([int min, int max])
```
Return a random number from Mersenne Twister

```
void mt_srand(int seed)
```
Seed Mersenne Twister random number generator

```
int rand([int min, int max])
```
Return a random number

```
void srand(int seed)
```
Seed random number generator

Semaphore Functions

```
int sem_acquire(int id)
```
Acquire the semaphore with the given id, blocking if necessary

```
int sem_get(int key [, int max_acquire [, int
perm]])
```
Return an ID for the semaphore with the given key, and allow max_acquire (default 1) processes to acquire it simultaneously

```
int sem_release(int id)
```
Release the semaphore with the given ID

Shared Memory Functions

```
int shm_attach(int key, int memsize, int perm)
```
Create or open a shared memory segment

```
int shm_detach(int shm_id)
```
Disconnect from shared memory segment

```
mixed shm_get_var(int id, int variable_key)
```
Return a variable from shared memory

```
int shm_put_var(int shm_id, int variable_key,
mixed variable)
```
Insert or updates a variable in shared memory

```
int shm_remove(int key)
```
Remove a shared memory segment

```
int shm_remove_var(int id, int variable_key)
```
Remove a variable from shared memory

Spell-Checking Functions

These functions require the *aspell* library from *http://metal-ab.unc.edu/kevina/aspell/*. Note that you need a version that has a C-callable client library. Version 0.26 has it, while Versions 0.27 and 0.28 do not.

```
int aspell_check(aspell int,string word)
```
Check if word is valid

```
int aspell_check_raw(aspell int,string word)
```
Check if word is valid, ignoring case and without trying to trim it in any way

```
int aspell_new(string master[, string personal])
```
Load a dictionary

```
array aspell_suggest(aspell int,string word)
```
Return an array of suggestions

Miscellaneous Functions

```
int connection_aborted(void)
```
Return true if client disconnected

```
int connection_status(void)
```
Return the connection status bitfield

```
int connection_timeout(void)
```
Return true if script timed out

```
int dl(string extension_filename)
```
Load a PHP extension at runtime

```
bool extension_loaded(string)
```
Return true if the specified extension is loaded

```
void flush(void)
```
Flush the output buffer

```
int function_exists(string function_name)
```
Checks if a given function has been defined

```
object get_browser([string browser_name])
```
Get information about the capabilities of a browser

```
string get_current_user(void)
```
Get the name of the owner of the current PHP script

```
int getlastmod(void)
```
Get time of last page modification

```
int getmyinode(void)
```
Get the inode of the current script being parsed

```
int getmypid(void)
```
Get current process ID

```
int getmyuid(void)
```
Get PHP script owner's user ID

```
array getrusage([ int who ])
```
Return an array of usage statistics

```
int ignore_user_abort(boolean value)
```
Set whether to ignore a user abort event

```
int mail(string to, string subject, string
message [, string additional_headers])
```
Send an email message

```
void register_shutdown_function(string function_
name)
```
   Register a user-level function to be called on request
   termination

```
void sleep(int seconds)
```
   Delay for a given number of seconds

```
void usleep(int micro_seconds)
```
   Delay for a given number of microseconds

In a Nutshell Quick References

O'REILLY®

TO ORDER: **800-998-9938** • *order@oreilly.com* • *http://www.oreilly.com/*
OUR PRODUCTS ARE AVAILABLE AT A BOOKSTORE OR SOFTWARE STORE NEAR YOU.
FOR INFORMATION: **800-998-9938** • **707-829-0515** • *info@oreilly.com*